Designed in the USSR 1950–1989

Designed in the USSR 1950–1989

From the collection of the Moscow Design Museum

Foreword 6
Soviet Design 8
Citizen 10
State 102
World 170
Biographies 235
Index 237

Foreword

Justin McGuirk

It is enshrined in the collective consciousness of the West that the collapse of the Soviet Union was a failure of lifestyle as much as politics. According to this view, the tedium of Soviet consumer goods was a fatal flaw in the system, grinding down morale and stoking the desires of the Russian citizen for blue jeans and other trappings of American-style consumerism. You might call this the washing machine theory of history. When President Nixon suggested to Nikita Khrushchev, in the famous 'kitchen debate' at the 1959 *American National Exhibition* in Moscow, that it would be better to compete over washing machines than rockets, he was rubbing his counterpart's nose in the superiority of American products.

In her magisterial oral history of post-Soviet Russia, *Second-Hand Time* (2013), Svetlana Alexievich provides plenty of voices that support this particular perspective. One of her interviewees recalls people '[t]hrowing out everything old and Soviet, and replacing it with everything new and imported… Every conversation was sprinkled with words like "Panasonic", "Sony", "Philips"…' Yet many others are despondent, bewildered by having thrown away a noble social experiment – for what, blue jeans and a hundred types of salami? The choice is framed as that between a great country and a normal one. Normality won.

This was a country prepared to invest in the most heroic feats – a man in space – but not in everyday desires. And yet, the fact that it is somehow a truism that Soviet products were substandard ought to make one suspicious. Indeed, it may be a consequence of how assured we are in our opinions of 'Soviet design' that the subject has been so little studied. This is one of the few books on the topic. While not a revisionist history offering up a parade of unsung masterpieces, it does, however, assemble a landscape of everyday life in the USSR, and that is a valuable step towards understanding a period that is receding fast. Here are the vacuum cleaners, table lamps, radios, cigarette packets, film posters, coffee tins and toys – the minutiae of a lost civilization.

It is true that Communism as manifested in the USSR – centralized, bureaucratic and unconducive to competition – was not fertile ground for a rich material culture. It is also true that many Soviet products were copies of Western models. Notoriously, the Vyatka scooter was an imitation Vespa down to the very logo font. This parallel world of ersatz knock-offs was encouraged by Party dignitaries returning from foreign trips with souvenirs that they would drop off at the *konstruktorskoe buro* (design department) of the relevant factory so they could be reverse engineered.

The All-Union Scientific Research Institute for Technical Aesthetics (VNIITE) did its best to foment a dynamic design culture, spearheaded by the journal *Technical Aesthetics*, but they were working against the grain of an economic system that was not geared up for stylistic variety. With Five Year Plans and production targets, factory directors were loath to retool the production line just because VNIITE had a better design up its sleeve.

One might argue that the system had its virtues. After all, Western materialism depends on a culture of disposability, bewildering choice, rapid obsolescence and keeping up with the Joneses. By comparison, the Soviet system was admirably sustainable: *avos'ki* fish-net shopping bags are vastly preferable to plastic ones, as are collapsible cups for use in drinking fountains compared to the insanity of plastic bottles. And those Space Age vacuum cleaners were nothing if not durable. But just as invidious comparison makes Western consumers feel inadequate, so it gnawed away at Russians with one eye on life across the Iron Curtain.

The domestic world of *Homo sovieticus*, as Alexievich calls pre-Yeltsin Russians, is laid out in these pages – at least in part. It is a collection worthy of closer scrutiny, one that may be as curious to Russians born after 1991 as it is to those in the West. When these items went on display at the Moscow Design Museum in 2012, the exhibition received 150,000 visitors. That is a sizeable audience for a group of objects that would have been utterly mundane only a generation ago. The question is, what was the appeal? Was it fascination for a time that now feels impossibly distant, or nostalgia for a country that once placed less stock in material things?

Soviet Design: Preserving the History

Alexandra Sankova, Moscow Design Museum

Throughout its complex history, Russia has experienced a number of major upheavals. A ruling party changes hands, the political landscape shifts and, soon after, entire belief systems, ways of life and cultural movements come under fire. This process, in turn, results in new discoveries and a re-shuffling of societal norms. For example, the Constructivists of the early twentieth century, who created a visual and substantive image of their new age of revolution, were effectively erased from Russia's collective memory when Socialist Realism was introduced as state policy in the 1930s. A similar fate befell many great Soviet designers following the collapse of the Soviet Union, when the industrial sector suffered catastrophic decline and countless important documents were lost or destroyed.

This curious feature of Russia's historical consciousness, with its attempts to eradicate and censor the past, was one of the reasons why, in 2012, the Moscow Design Museum – an institution dedicated to the preservation of Russia's design heritage – decided to hold an exhibition on Soviet design from the 1950s to the 1980s. It was the institute's first exhibition, and the aim was to acknowledge the individuals behind the wealth of anonymous objects populating the USSR – items which, decades later, can still be found in innumerable homes and workplaces across the region.

During the Soviet era, there existed a veritable army of professional designers who were mentioned only on payslips and industrial certificates. In contrast to their Western counterparts, these were not public figures. Instead, manufacturers employed so-called 'artistic engineers' who were responsible for the visual appearance of their products. There were 'sample product rooms', where Western examples of industrial products were displayed, often serving as prototypes for their Soviet equivalents. They were studied in detail, adapted to available technology and put into mass production. Hard as it is to imagine now, the words 'design' and 'designer' were banned until as late as the 1980s.

This extraordinary lexical gap, which designers had to live with for decades, nevertheless encouraged the development of innovative conceptual projects. In 1962, the Council of Ministers of the Soviet Union ordered the creation of the All-Union Scientific Research Institute for Technical Aesthetics (VNIITE), which comprised a head office in Moscow and ten branches within major cities across the USSR. The main objective of this new organization was to improve the quality of mass-produced industrial goods through the aid of design. Under the leadership of chief designer Yuri Soloviev, VNIITE took on not only the implementation of these goals, but also the development of a theoretical and practical framework for the entire system of design. With this new structure came the regulation of the design profession, the establishment of quality standards and assessment criteria, the publication of monthly journal *Technical Aesthetics* and the compilation of an extensive library of design publications.

The network of cooperation was vast, with a number of other specialist research and design organizations working under the supervision of VNIITE. These included the Experimental Research Institute for Toys, the All-Union Institute for Furniture Design and Technology, the All-Union Institute for Light and the Scientific Research Institute for Art, as well as a group of Special Artistic Engineering Bureaus (SKhKBs). The initiative also brought together people from the most diverse professions, including philosophers, culture specialists, art critics and historians, architects, engineers and, of course, designers. Its status as a separate institute made it effectively a state within a state. Over time the institute was able to form its own scientific school of thought, under which Western principles of commercial design had to be adapted to fit socialist ideology, the state-planned economy and unique geographic and political conditions of the Soviet Union.

This system of design survived right up until the collapse of the USSR, and during the subsequent period of transition, President Boris Yeltsin signed an order for it to be revived. However, his appeal did not come to fruition. The next generation of designers in the 1990s were quicker to adapt and survive in the difficult economic circumstances, without the need to follow in the footsteps of their predecessors. While certain areas of design flourished, particularly graphic design, the industrial sector and its socialist ideology gradually deteriorated.

Over time, piece by piece, the Moscow Design Museum has acquired a vast collection of products, graphics and documents, which together will help to plug the gaps in this largely undocumented stretch of history. We are now living in an era when profound changes to the socio-political structure of society are influencing the environment in which design takes place. However, this makes it all the more interesting for the current generation to reveal the distinctive voice and vision behind this overlooked age, its particular personal experience and different global goals.

Drawing back the Iron Curtain, *Designed in the USSR: 1950–1989* explores this extraordinary period, when function and utility were the driving forces behind ideas but remarkable examples innovation and creativity still flourished. Organized visually, and with commentary captions throughout, the book is broken down into three chapters. The first, 'Citizen', celebrates the everyday, domestic and consumer products that relate to an individual's wants or needs: the iconic children's roly-poly dolls, or *Nevalyashka* – round, red, cherub-faced toys, which, no matter how hard they're pushed, always return to an upright position [p. 82]; the hazardous, fuse-blowing, boiling wand [p. 76], essentially a mobile immersion heater and a must-have for every Soviet traveller. The second chapter, 'State', focuses on items that reveal something about the state-controlled system of design: a dial-less telephone that offered a direct line of communication between top-ranking employees and party officials [p. 129]; a children's modular radio construction kit, for the aspiring young spy [p. 109]. The final chapter, 'World', takes the Soviet Union out of the Eastern Bloc and on to the international stage: we have Misha the Bear, the 1980 Moscow Olympic Games mascot [pp. 176–7], the first to be drawn in full-face, rather than profile, in order to build an emotional connection with viewers; then the Saturnas vacuum cleaner [p. 193], a remarkable example of space-age design, inspired – like many things at that time – by the Sputnik satellite.

Through these different lenses, readers are taken on a micro-to-macro tour of the practical, kitsch, playful, politicized and often avant-garde designs, compiled to create a unique and compelling view into life in the USSR.

CITIZEN

01

02

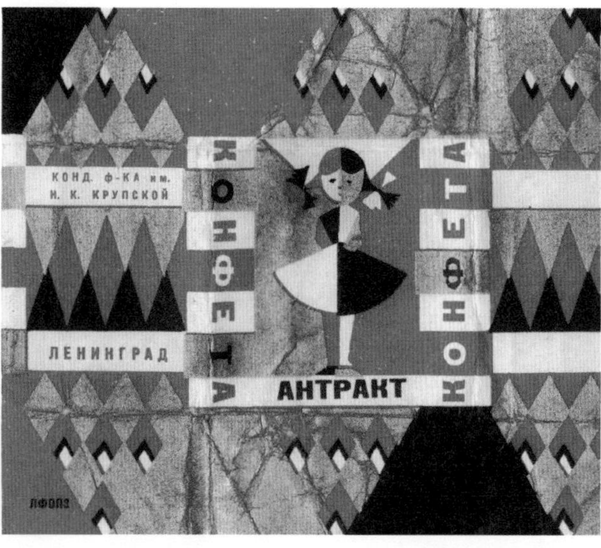

03

04

01 **Tuzik** sweet wrapper, 1960–70s. Manufactured by the Novosibirsk Chocolate Factory.

02 **Vosmoe Marta** (8 March, International Women's Day) sweet wrapper, 1960–70s. Manufactured by the Konkordiya Samoylova Confectionery Factory.

03 **Antract** (Intermission) sweet wrapper, 1960–70s. Manufactured by the Nadezhda Krupskaya Confectionery Factory.

04 **Belochka** (Squirrel) sweet wrapper, 1960–70s. Manufactured by the Nalchik Confectionery Factory.

05

05 **Sport** Aeroflot Airlines sweet wrapper, 1960s.

06

06 **Sport** sweet wrapper, 1960s. Manufactured by the Leningrad Confectionery Factory.

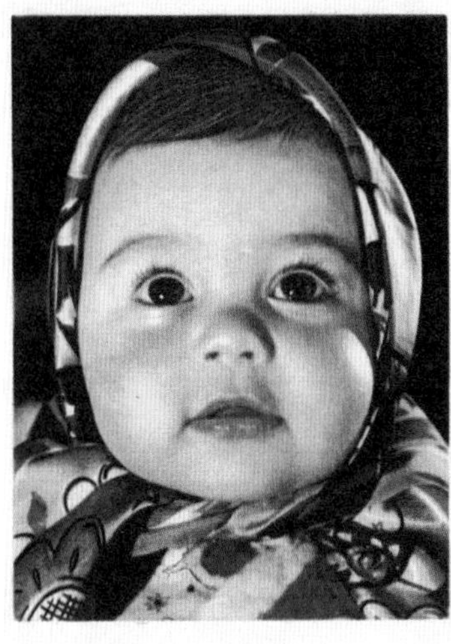

07

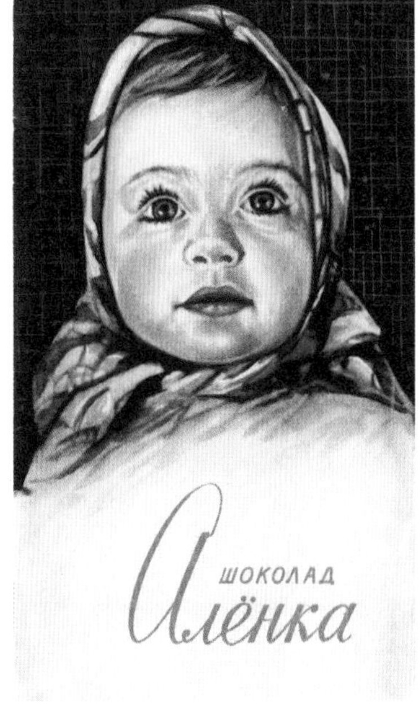

08

09

10

07 **Postcard** with photograph of Elena Gerinas, 1966.

08–10 **Alyonka** chocolate wrappers, 1960–70s. Manufactured by the Krasny Oktyabr (Red October) Chocolate Factory. The packaging for the Alyonka chocolate bar is the most prolific example of Soviet branding designed in the Socialist Realist style and is still produced in its original form today. The touching portrait of a little girl in a head scarf was made in 1966 by Nikolai Maslov, an artist working at the Red October factory. The portrait's original inspiration came from Elena Gerinas, whose photo was submitted by her father, photojournalist Alexander Gerinas, for a competition held by the *Evening Moscow* newspaper.

11

11 **Mir** (World Peace) sweet wrapper, 1950–70s. Manufactured by the Nadezhda Krupskaya Confectionery Factory.

12

13

14

15

12 **Kara-Kum** chocolate wrapper, 1950–70s. Manufactured by the Nizhniy Tagil Confectionery Factory.

13 **Lakomka** sweet wrapper, 1950–70s. Manufactured by the Perm Confectionery Factory.

14 **Mokko** sweet wrapper, 1950–70s. Manufactured by the Blagoveshensk Confectionery Union.

15 **Meteor** sweet wrapper, 1960–70s. Manufactured by the Kemerovo Confectionery Factory.

16

17

18

19

16–17 **Tuzik** chocolate wrappers, 1950–70s. Manufactured by the Novosibirsk Chocolate Factory.

18 **Petushok Zolotoy Grebeshok** (Rooster with a Golden Crest) chocolate wrapper, 1950–70s. Manufactured by the Pyotr Babayev Confectionery Factory.

19 **Veseli Zoosad** (Funny Zoo) chocolate wrapper, 1950–70s. Manufactured by the First Leningrad Confectionery Factory.

20

20 **Mishka Na Severe** (Bear at the North Pole) chocolate wrapper, 1950–70s.

21

21 **Leningrad** chocolate wrapper, 1960s. Manufactured by the Nadezhda Krypskaya Confectionery Factory.

22

23

24

25

22 **Salut** (Fireworks) chocolate wrapper, 1960–70s. Manufactured by the Sverdlovsk Confectionery Factory.
23 **Leningrad** chocolate wrapper, 1960s. Manufactured by the Nadezhda Krypskaya Confectionery Factory.

24 – 25 **Sport** sweet wrappers, 1950s. Manufactured by the Anastas Mikoian Confectionery Factory.

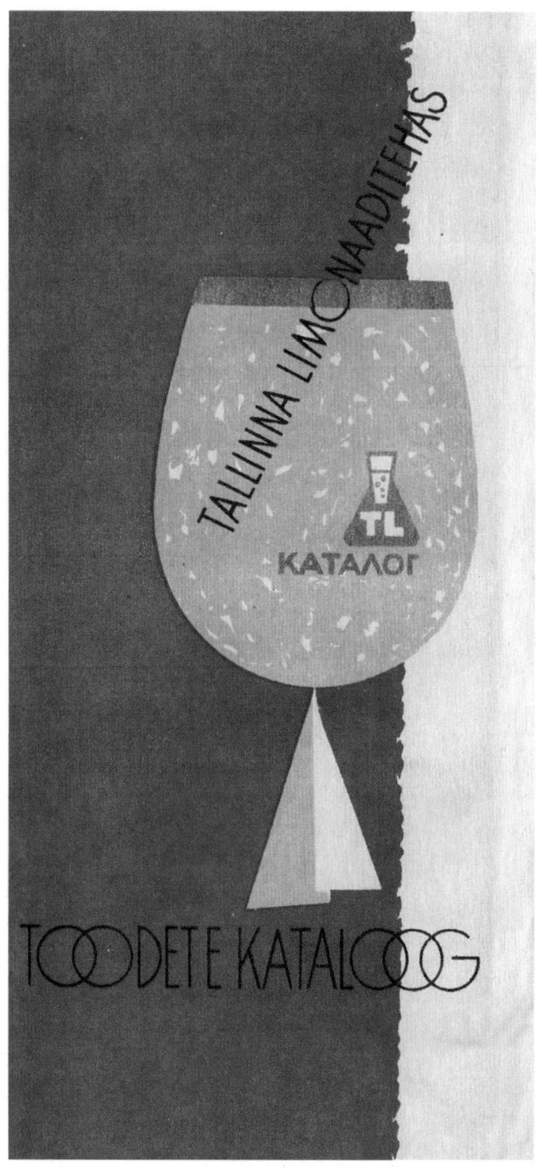

26

27

26 – 29 **Promotional brochures** for Estonian soft drinks, 1960s. Manufactured by the Tallinn Soft Drink Factory.

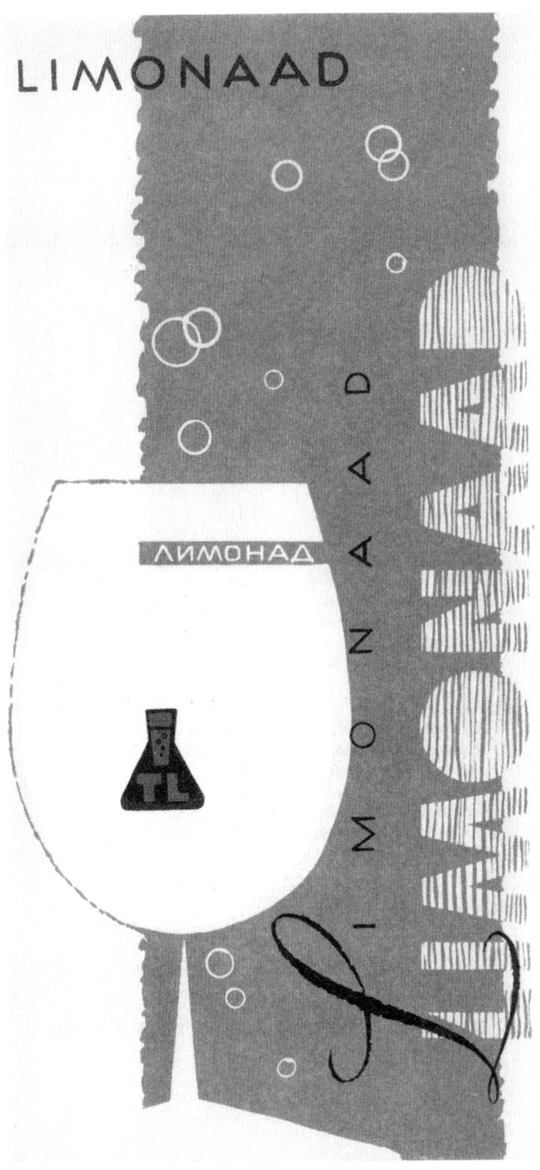
LIMONAAD
ЛИМОНАД
TL
LIMONAAD

28

TL
JOOGID
VÄRSKENDAVAD
ЛИМОНАД
LIMONAAD
TL
0,33L

29

30

31

30 **Tetrahedron-shaped milk carton**, 1959–90s. Manufactured by the Ostankino Dairy Combine. In 1959, the Soviet Union bought the technology for producing tetrahedron-shaped milk cartons from the Swedish company Tetra Pak. At that time, European consumers were already using plastic shopping bags that were susceptible to damage from the sharp edges of pyramidal packages. The Soviets, however, continued to carry their groceries in convenient *avos' ki* (just-in-case) string bags, allowing the technology to remain in use for many years. The package's abstract pattern of red and blue triangles and the inscription in geometric san-serif is a characteristic example of Khrushchev era Modernist design that reinterpreted the ideas of Russian Constructivism.

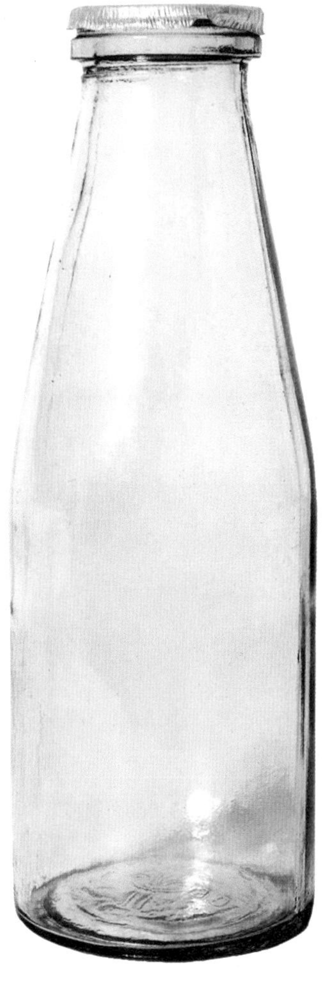

32

31 **Sgushchonka** (Condensed Milk) label, 1930s. Manufactured by the Rogachev Dairy and Cannery Combine. The famous white-and-blue pattern of the Sgushchonka label was designed by Iraida Fomina, whose geometric composition reflected the spirit of Soviet Art Deco while the lettering was typical of Russian Constructivism. This memorable design has remained unchanged for more than eighty years.

32 **Dairy bottle with aluminium caps**, 1960–90s. Soviet wide-neck dairy bottles are a successful example of sustainable design. Their contents, such as milk, kefir and *ryazhenka* (fermented milk), was indicated by the colour of the foil cap. Fully recyclable and with no label attached, the bottles required minimal resources and have come to represent important trends in contemporary packaging design.

Everyday work is a step towards Communism.

Каждый день труда – шаг к коммунизму.

33

34

35

36

33 **Caviar tin**, 1970s. Manufactured by the Gurievsk Fish and Cannery Combine. Tins were a common type of packaging in the Soviet Union – since 1937, more than 700 types of tinned goods have been produced. Most popular were salmon, caviar, crabs and *tushonka* (stewed meat). In addition, tins and boxes were used for storing tea, coffee, cocoa, confectionery and the ever-popular condensed milk.

34 **Detski** children's tooth powder, 1959–77. Manufactured by the Kuybyshev Perfume Combine.

35 **Chai Krasnodarsky Extra** Krasnodar extra-quality tea tin, 1960s.

36 **Chai Gruzinsky Extra** Georgian extra-quality tea tin, 1950s.

37

37 **Kreker K Zavtraku** breakfast crackers box, 1970s.
Manufactured by the Bolshevik Factory.

38

38 **Rozhki** pasta packaging, 1980s. Manufactured by the Rostov Pasta Factory.

39

39 **Coffee grinder** with packaging, 1970–80s.
Manufactured by the Drafting Equipment Plant.

40

41

42

40–42 **Instant coffee tins**, 1970s.

43

43 **Souvenir paper bag** from the World Festival of Youth and Students, 1957.

44

45

46

44–45 **Confectionery tins** with folk motifs, 1970–80s.
46 **Troika** (Three Horses) assorted confectionery box, 1981. Manufactured by the Sormovsk Confectionery Factory. Starting in the late 1960s there was a renewed interest in traditional folk culture in the Soviet Union. Considerable numbers of picture books were published featuring examples of folk and applied art from different regions in the USSR. Packaging designs often drew inspiration from the characters of *byliny* (Russian traditional epic poems) – young women in folk costumes, elements of wooden and stone architecture and traditional peasant crafts – which were then adapted for modern graphic styles and techniques.

47

48

49

50

47 **Salhino** Georgian wine label, 1960–80s.
48 **Ereti** Georgian wine label, 1960–80s.
49 **Chvanchkara** Georgian wine label, 1960–80s.
50 **Tvishi** Georgian wine label, 1960–80s.

51

51 **Tetra** Georgian wine label, 1960–80s.

52

53

54

55

52 **Mukuzani** Georgian wine label, 1960–80s.
53 **Cinandali** Georgian wine label, 1960–80s.
54 **Sovetskoe Champanskoe** Soviet 'Champagne' label, 1937. Designed by Alexander Mandrysov.
55 **Saperavi** Georgian wine label, 1960–80s.

56

57

56 – 57 **Rkacitelli** wine labels, 1960–70s.

58

59

60

61

58–60 **Dagvino** souvenier Cognac boxes, 1960–70s. The labels for the popular Dagvino brand of Dagestani brandies and wines were designed by David Lanovskii and Anna Fokina, artists of the Souzprodoformlenie design house. Their elegant graphic style is based on the ornamental traditions of the region. Lanovskii and Fokina were awarded the title of Honorary Art Figures of Dagestan in recognition of their work.

61 **Zolotoy Yarlyk** (Gold Label) cocoa packaging, 1960–80s. Manufactured by the Krasny Oktyabr Chocolate Factory.

62

62 **Khoziaistvennie** household matchbox, 1980s.
Manufactured by the Gigant Match Factory.

63

63 **Zolotoe Koltso** (Golden Ring) hand-coloured design template for a beer can, 1979. Designed by Kirill Sukhanov. The first Soviet brand of canned beer, Zolotoe Koltso was developed for guests of the forthcoming Moscow Olympics. Drawing on historical imagery, Sukhanov depicted a coat of arms using regional icons from the cities of the Golden Ring (a group of ancient cities northeast of Moscow that are popular tourist destinations). Each of the illustrations was outlined to resemble old engravings. The beer can was made of tin and could only be opened using a tin opener.

64

64 **Stolichnaya** (Capital) vodka labels for export, 1947. The original Stolichnaya label design is understood to have been developed by Vladimir Yakovlev. However, artist Andrei Iogansen also claims copyright for the drawing. The label depicts the Hotel Moskva, built in the centre of the Soviet capital from 1933–5, and is a vivid example of the transition from Constructivist to Stalinist architecture. The print quality and detailing is notably better on the export bottles, whereas the pattern was simplified for domestic use.

65

66

65 **Pshenichnaya** (Wheat) vodka bottle, 1980–90s. Manufactured by Minpisheprom.
66 **Limonaya** (Lemon) bitter liqueur bottle, 1980–90s. Manufactured by the Kristal Factory.

67

67 **Prazdnichni Nabor** festive gift set for alcohol, 1956.
Manufactured by the Moscow Wine Factory.

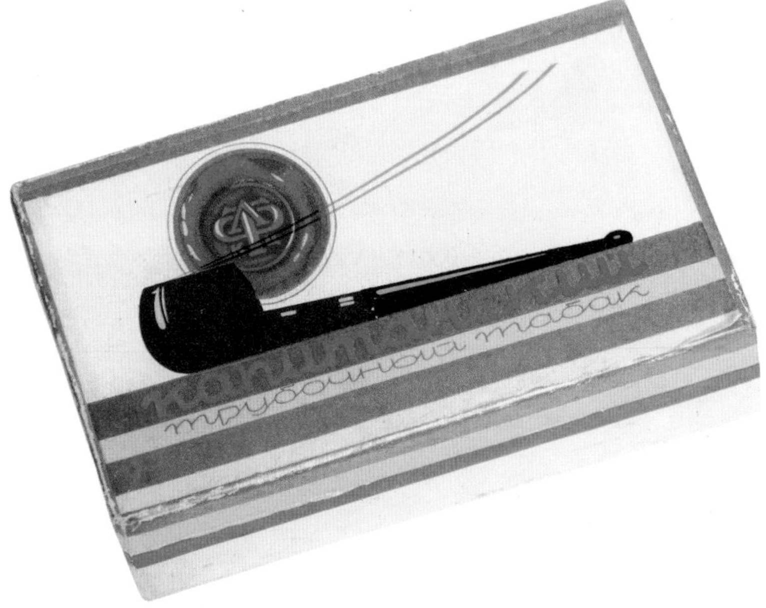

68

69

68 **Kapitanskiy** (Captain's) pipe tobacco packaging, 1950–60s. Manufactured by the Clara Tsetkin Tobacco Factory.
69 **Belaya Noch** (White Night) cigarette tin, 1960s. Manufactured by the Clara Tsetkin Tobacco Factory.

70

71

72

73

70 **Prima** cigarette packaging, 1970s.
71 **Polet** cigarette packaging, 1970–90s. Manufactured by the Yava Tobacco Factory.
72 **Moskva** (Moscow) cigar packaging, 1958–60s. Manufactured by the Pogar Cigarette and Cigar Factory.
73 **Yava** cigarette packaging, 1980s. Manufactured by the Yava Tobacco Factory.

74

75

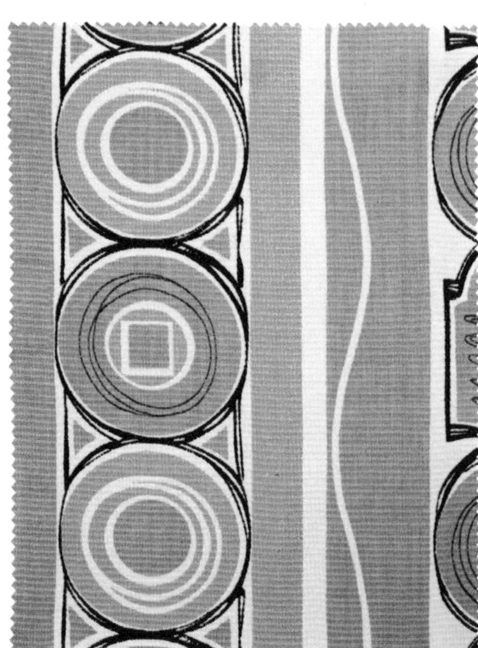
76

77

74 **Relief fabric swatch,** 1960s. Manufactured by the Trekhgornaya Textile Factory.
75 **Printed cotton fabric swatch,** 1960s. Manufactured by the Gori Cotton Combine.
76 **Relief fabric swatch,** 1960s. Manufactured by the Trekhgornaya Textile Factory.
77 **Heavy muslin fabric swatch,** 1960s. Manufactured by the Trekhgornaya Textile Factory.

78

78 **Heavy muslin fabric swatch**, 1960s. Manufactured by the Trekhgornaya Textile Factory.

79

79 **Printed cotton fabric swatch**, 1960s. Manufactured by the Ivanovo Cotton Combine.

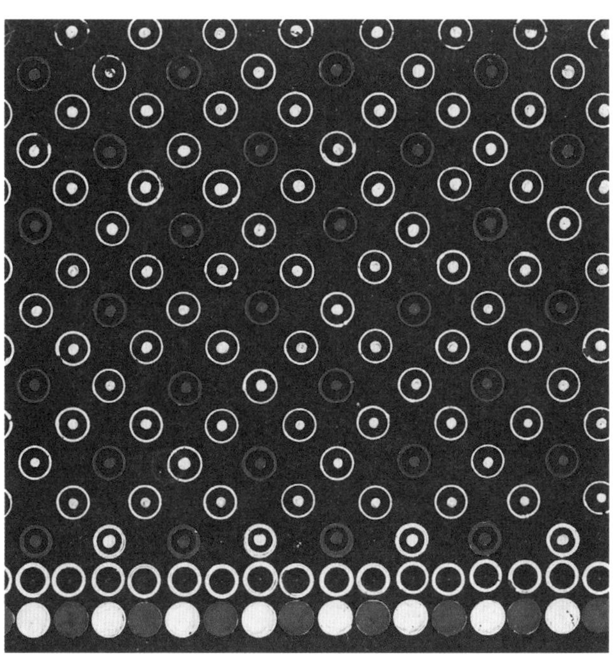

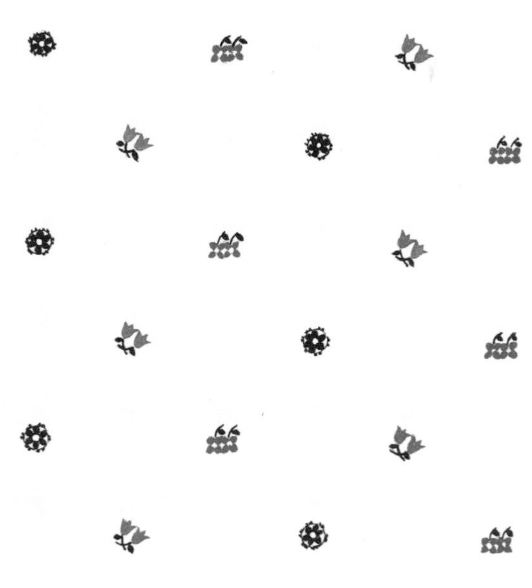

80

80 **Gouache drawings** for textile patterns, 1950–60s. Designed by Vera Sklyarova, manufactured by the Rosa Luxemburg Krasnaya Factory. Having graduated from the Moscow Textile Institute, Vera Sklyarova (1908–76) worked as a textile designer for many years. Following World War II, one in every five Soviet women owned a dress featuring one of her floral pattern designs. From 1957 to 1984 she worked as chief editor at the fashion magazine published by the USSR's All-Union Fashion House.

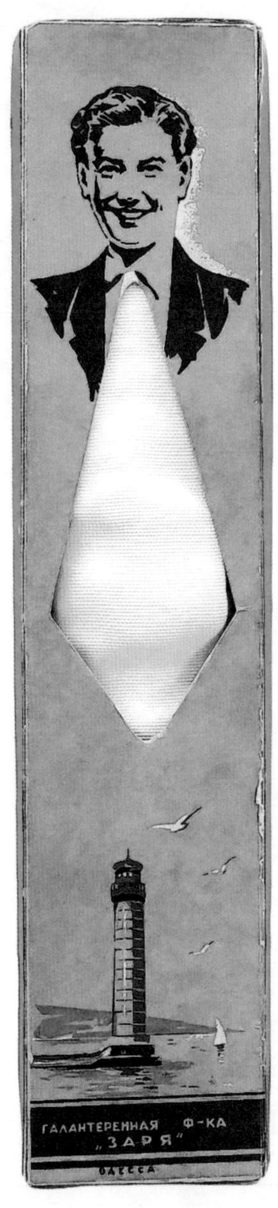

81

81 **White tie** in a box, 1950s. Manufactured by the Novaya Zarya (New Dawn) Perfume and Cosmetics Factory.

82

82 **Krasnaya Moskva** (Red Moscow) perfume bottle and packaging, 1970–80s. Manufactured by the Novaya Zarya Perfume and Cosmetics Factory. Red Moscow perfume is a famous fragrance from the Soviet era. It is believed to have been created by French perfumer Auguste Michel on the basis of Le Bouquet Préféré de l'Impératrice (Empress' Favourite Bouquet), which was dedicated to the House of Romanov in 1913. Andrei Evseev developed the first design for the bottle and box, combining graphic elements of both old and new styles: golden tendrils à la Art Nouveau and a Constructivist geometric pattern. Over time, the style of the bottle and its packaging have evolved, with a more modern design adopted in the 1970s.

83

83 **Natasha and Sasha** perfume packaging, 1970–90s. Manufactured by the Novaya Zarya Perfume and Cosmetics Factory. The affordable technique of printing photographs on paper, cardboard and metal packaging appeared in the USSR in the 1970s. This image of a tanned blonde girl with a fashionable haircut was printed on packages of cologne, perfume and soap. The portrait was taken from an East German photo bank while the model, as it turned out, was of Finnish origin. A men's perfume called Sasha was also produced, but its packaging was never as popular as that of the Finnish beauty. The factory even received love letters addressed to Natasha.

84

85

86

87

84 **Skazka O Tsare Saltane** (Tale of Tsar Saltan) perfume bottle, 1960s. Manufactured by the Novaya Zarya Perfume and Cosmetics Factory.

85 **Kamenniy Tsvetok** (Stone Flower) perfume bottle and packaging, 1950s. Manufactured by the Novaya Zarya Perfume and Cosmetics Factory.

86 **Ballet** face powder box, 1950–60s. Manufactured by the Novaya Zarya Perfume and Cosmetics Factory.

87 **Krasnaya Moskva** (Red Moscow) face powder box, 1930–50s. Designed by Andrei Evseev, manufactured by the Novaya Zarya Perfume and Cosmetics Factory.

88

89

90

91

88 **Dymok** (Smoke) perfume bottle, 1970s. Manufactured by the Alie Parusa (Scarlet Sails) Perfume and Cosmetics Combine.
89 **Skazka O Tsare Saltane** (Tale of Tsar Saltan) perfume packaging, 1960s. Manufactured by the Novaya Zarya Perfume and Cosmetics Factory.
90 **Dymok** perfume bottle, 1970s. Manufactured by the Alie Parusa Perfume and Cosmetics Combine.
91 **Perfume bottle** with atomizer, 1960–80s.

92

93

92 **Sputnik** wind-up shaver packaging, 1968. Manufactured by the Leningrad Patefon Factory. This design was based on the Thorens Riviera wind-up shaver from Switzerland and was produced with only slight modifications until the 1980s.

93 **Pudra-Listochki** face powder in sheets, cosmetics packaging, 1960s. Manufactured by VTO.

94

SOVIET LIFE
September 1966
• 35 cents
Vyacheslav
Zaitsev:
A Russian
Yves
St. Laurent

95

96

97

98

99

94 **Zhurnal Mod** magazine, Spring 1966.

95 **Soviet Life** magazine, September 1966. This limited-edition magazine, published monthly by the Embassy of the USSR in the USA, reported on Soviet life and culture. In turn, from 1956 to 1991, *America* magazine was published in the Soviet Union. The fashion sketches on the cover were designed by Vyacheslav Zaitsev for a collection that became a big success in Vancouver in 1969. Zaitsev was one of the first fashion designers who successfully combined key European trends with Russian traditional costumes. The issue's headline reads: 'Vyacheslav Zaitsev: A Russian Yves St. Laurent'.

96–99 **Odezhda I Bit** (Clothes and Household) magazine, 1963–5.

100

101

102

103

100–101 **Modeli Odezhdi** (Models of Clothing) magazine, 1968. Illustrations by the Leningrad House of Clothing Models. In the Soviet Union, high-end clothing wasn't available in regular stores; it could only be bought in either Section No. 200 of GUM (a State Department Store) or in the Beryozka (Little Birch Tree) chain of stores. Section No. 200 was opened in 1953 and served only party leaders and members of their families; the Beryozka chain of stores opened in 1962 and sold goods in exchange for special certificates equivalent to the US dollar. Ordinary citizens had to make clothes themselves using sewing patterns from fashion magazines or buy them on the black market.

102 **Modi Tkani** (Textile Fashions) magazine, 1967.

104

105

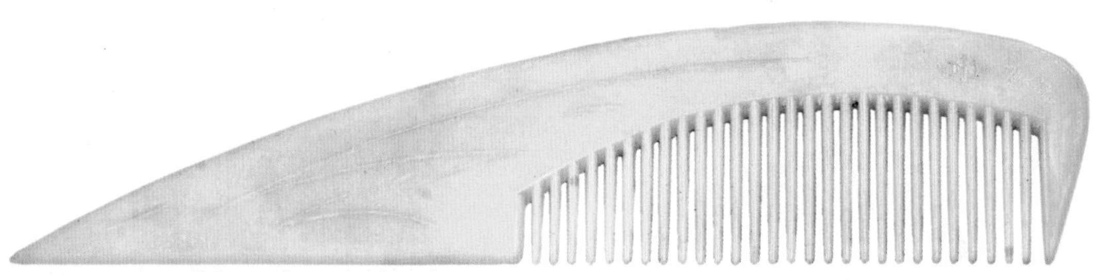

106

103 **Zhurnal Mod** magazine, No. 2, 1960. During the Khrushchev 'thaw' period, international fashion trends started to filter through to the Soviet Union, thanks largely to the 1957 World Festival of Youth and Students and the 1959 Christian Dior show in Moscow. The model on the cover of this magazine shows off a new silhouette, typical of the time.

104 **Handbag**, 1950s. Manufactured by the Factory of Leather Goods.

105 **Lipstick jewellery box** with embedded mirror, 1971. Prototype designed by Svetlana Mirzoyan. Although this model never was mass-produced, it was used as a prop in the movie *Tiatr* (*Theatre*) in 1978.

106 **Comb**, 1960s.

107

107 **Sewing supplies box**, 1970–80s.

108

108 **Skorokhod** (Fast Walker) shoes label, 1950s. Manufactured by the Yakov Kalinin Shoe Factory.
109 **Evening shoes** with fur pompom, limited edition, 1980s. Designed and manufactured at the All-Union Fashion House.
110 **Wooden platform** with textile and leatherette strap, 1970s.

109

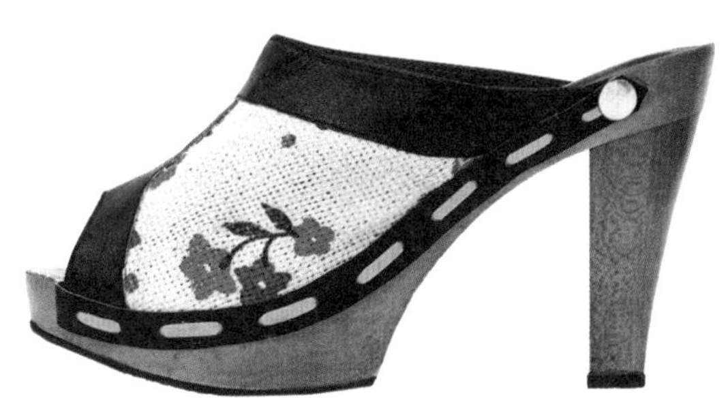

110

111

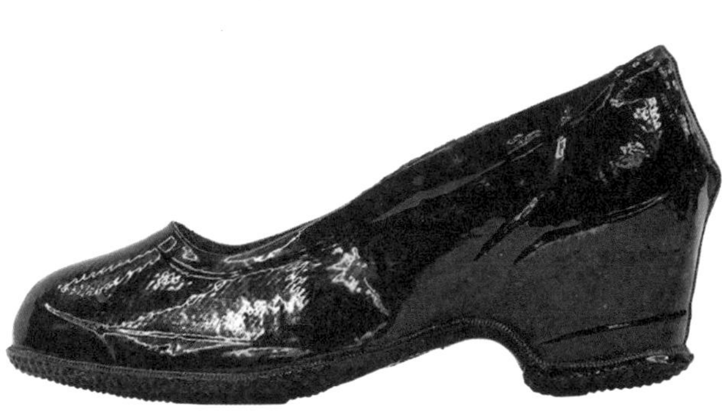

112

111 **Suede evening ankle boots**, limited edition, 1980s. Designed and manufactured at the All-Union Fashion House. This pair of ankle boots belonged to Soviet actress and singer Tatyana Shmyga. Many shoes made in the USSR were designed and produced as limited editions and only accessible to the Soviet elite. Due to this scarcity, those imported from Poland, Czechoslovakia, East Germany and Hungary were in high demand.

112 **Women's medium-heel galoshes**, 1950–80s. Manufactured by the Krasny Bogatir Factory. Galoshes were extremely popular in the USSR. The wide range of models included men's, women's and children's; flat, high or medium-heel; and those with or without a warm fabric lining – virtually all demographics and life situations. Due to the lack of athletic footwear, pointed-toe galoshes were popular with Soviet mountain climbers.

113

113 **Ceramic sugar bowl** with abstract geometric pattern, 1960s. Manufactured by the Mikhail Lomonosov Porcelain Factory.

114 **Ceramic vase** with abstract pattern, 1960s.

115 **Ceramic vase** with wavy-line pattern, 1960s. Manufactured by the Leningrad Porcelain Plant.

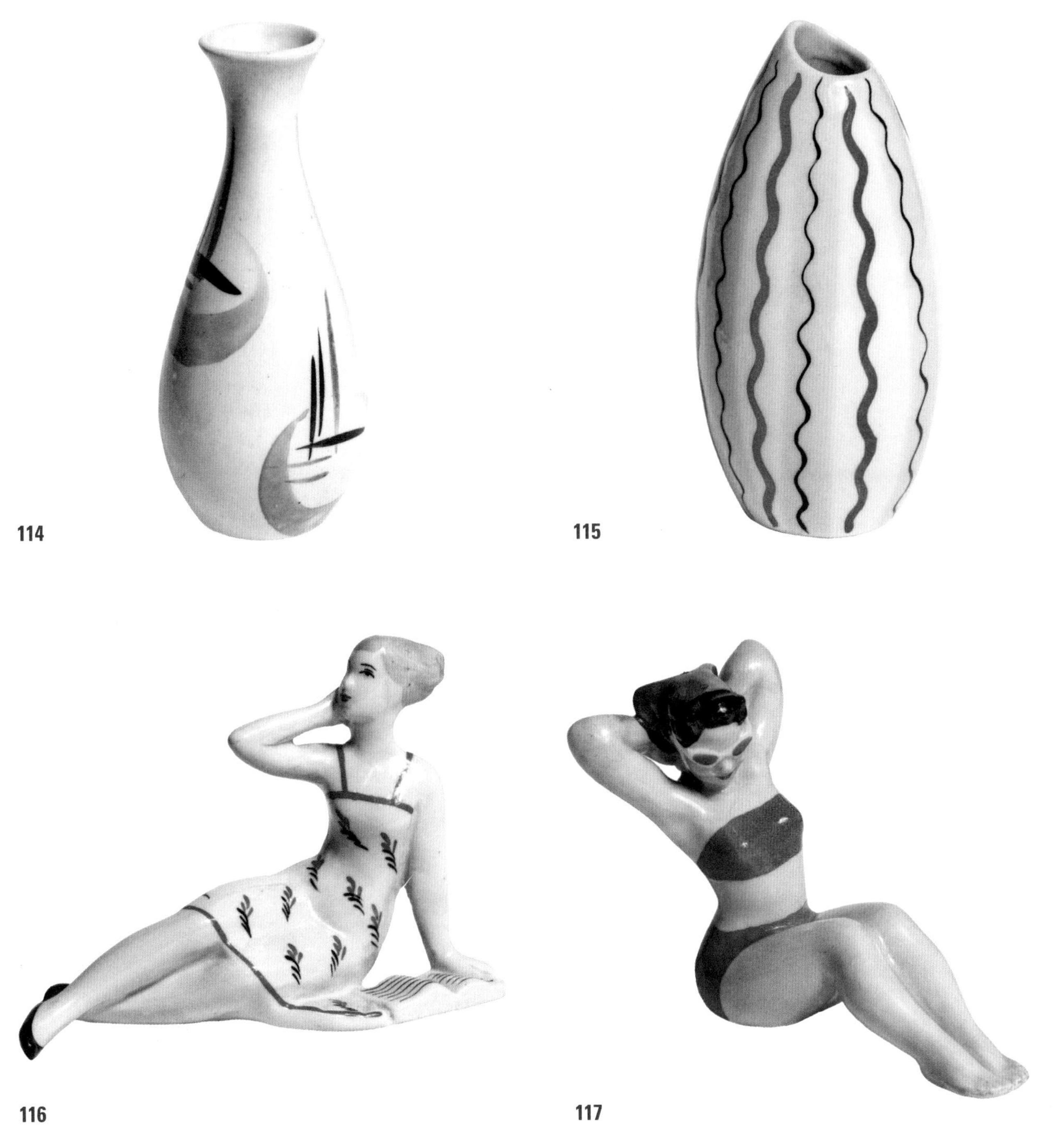

114

115

116

117

116 **Devushka S Knigoi** (Girl with a Book) ceramic figurine, 1963. Designed by S I Weinstein-Mashurina, manufactured by the Sysert Ceramic Factory. Between the 1950s and 1980s, factory-employed ceramic artists based their designs on national ornaments, folk motifs and modern geometrical patterns. Figurines depicting leisure time activities and everyday life were very popular and could be found in most Soviet homes.

117 **Beach series** ceramic figurine, 1959. Designed by Olga Rapay, manufactured by the Kiev Experimental Artistic Ceramics Plant, Polonia Plant of Artistic Ceramics and Kiev Porcelain Factory.

118

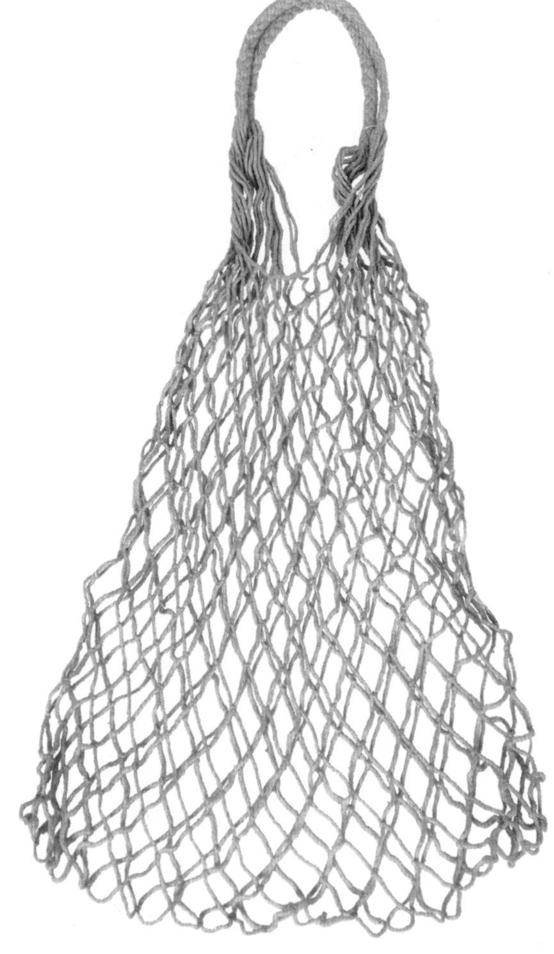

119

118 **Household plastic bag**, 1970s.

119 **Avos´ka** string shopping bag, 1950–80s. These string shopping bags were widely used during Soviet times. They were produced at the factories of the All-Union Society of the Blind and were commonly known as *avos'ki* – a word derived from the adverb *avos'* meaning 'just in case' and expressing hope for something. When folded, they fit into pockets, making them easy to have at hand if people spotted scarce or valuable goods. They could also be washed and were extremely durable. The *avoska* went out of use in the 1980s when it was replaced by disposable plastic bags. However, the current move towards increased sustainability has now brought these iconic bags back into fashion.

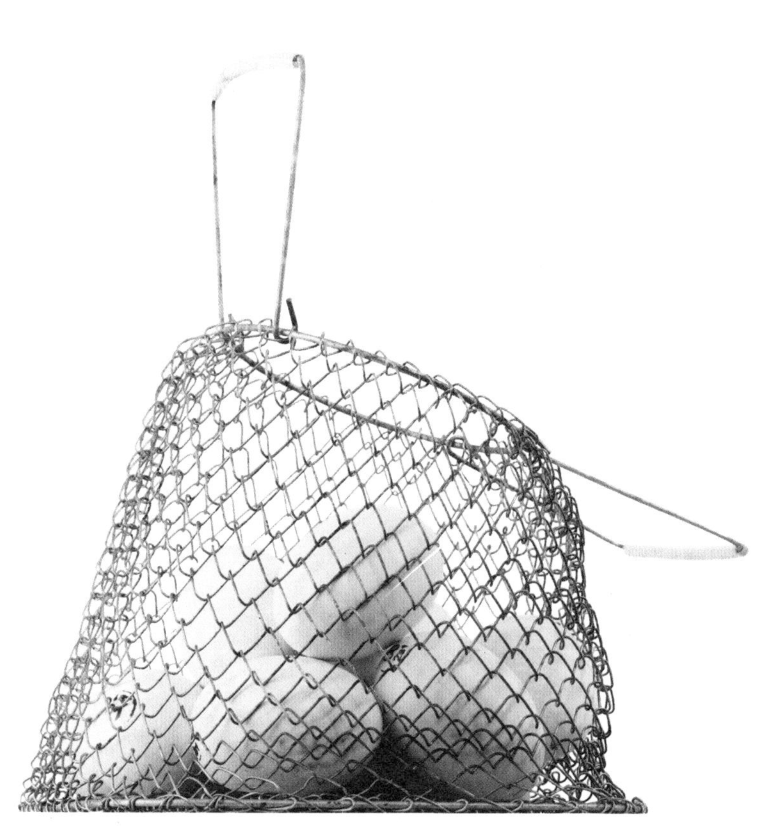

120

121

120 **Metal egg carrier**, 1970–80s.
121 **Soda siphon**, 1960–70s.

122

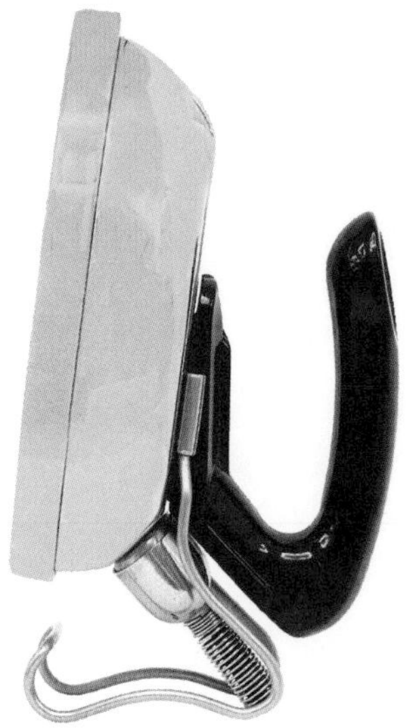

123

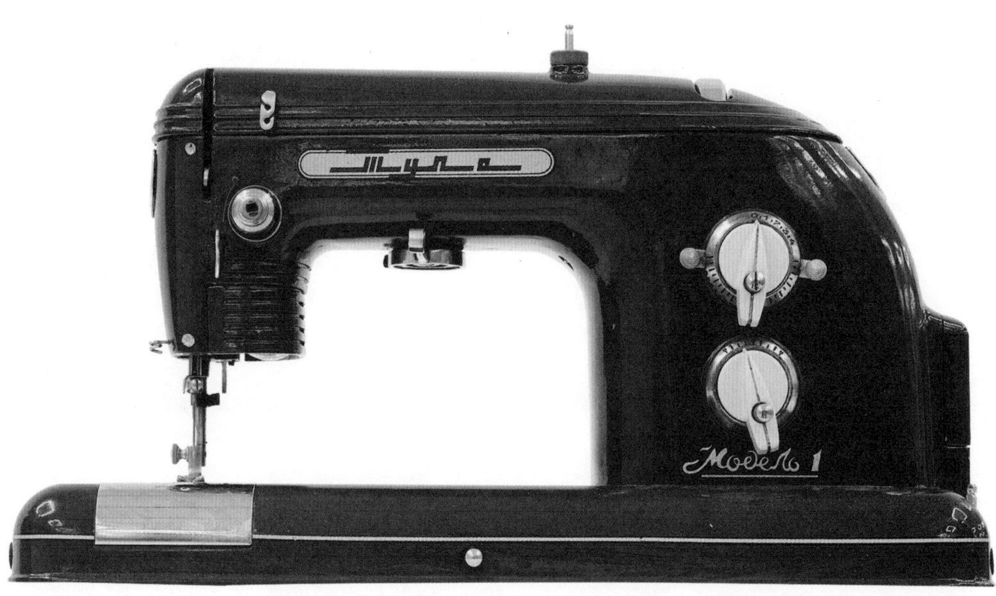

124

122 **UE4** portable iron, 1967. Manufactured by the Kharkov Electromechanical Plant.

123 **Electric iron**, 1956. Manufactured by the Kharkov Electromechanical Plant.

124 **Tula** sewing machine, 1955. Manufactured by the Tula Mechanical Engineering Plant. Tula was one of the first sewing machines in the USSR that featured an electric drive. It was rather heavy, being made of chrome-plated steel, and the design of its pins and overlocks were based on those of German sewing machines. Since there was a shortage of basic consumer goods, especially clothing, sewing machines were extremely useful. Although the Tula was relatively popular and extensively advertised, most Soviet citizens preferred the trusted Zinger (Singer) hand sewing machines.

125

125 **Riga 60** washing machine, 1960. Manufactured by the Riga Electric Engineering Plant.

As you want, so you must work.

Как работал, так и заработал.

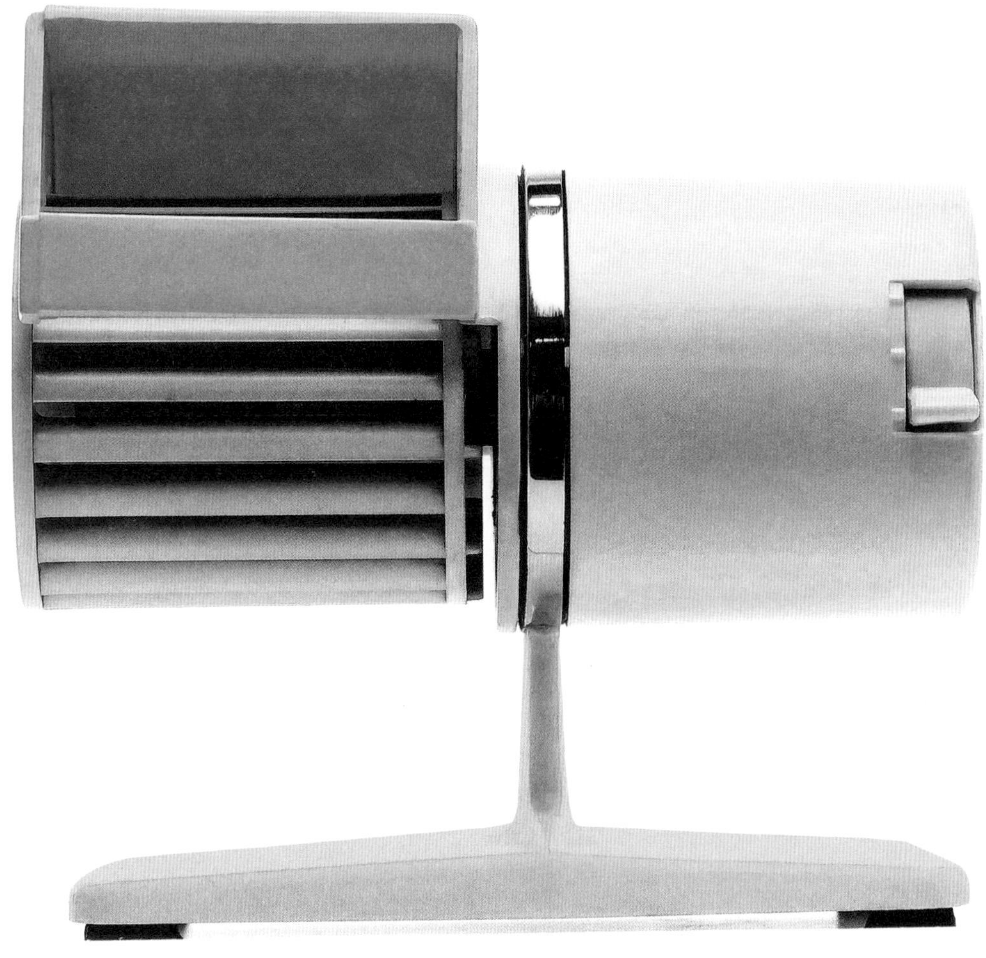

126

126 **VN10 UP4** desk fan, 1978. This model was based on the Braun 1961 HL1 desk fan, designed by Reinhold Weiss. Weiss worked as the deputy designer at Braun, under design director Dieter Rams.

127

128

127–128 **Metal table lamps**, 1960s.

129

129 **Wall light prototype**, 1969. Manufactured by the Riga Lighting Engineering Plant. Svetlana Mirzoyan designed this wall light while working at the VNIITE Specialized Design Bureau (SHKB) in Riga. The manufacturer didn't have the proper equipment needed to produce the spherical form for the light's reflector, so Mirzoyan repurposed metal components from teapots produced at another plant. This innovative thinking helped to turn her idea into reality and introduce a new wall light model.

130

130 **Tabletop scale**, 1960–70s.

131

132

133

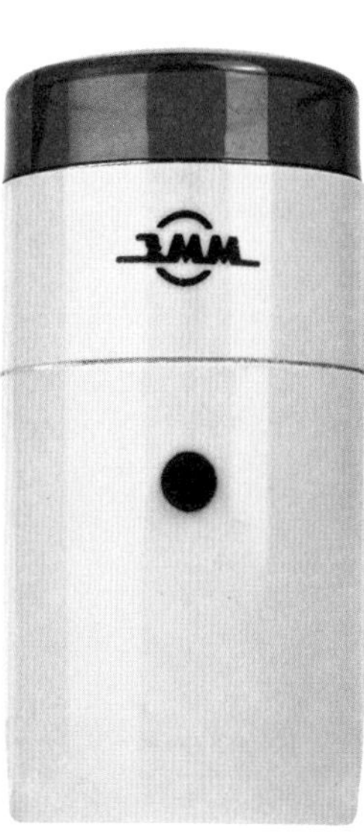

134

131 **Enamel container** with the World Festival of Youth and Students emblem, 1985.
132 **Plastic thermos**, 1980s.
133 **Rice and raisin tins** for dry goods, 1970–80s.
134 **ZMM** electric coffee grinder, 1970–80s. Manufactured by the Moscow Micro-Machine Factory. Similarly to the VN10 UP4 desk fan [p. 71], this model was based on an existing Braun product – the 1967 KSM 1/11 coffee grinder, designed by Reinhold Weiss.

135

136

135 **Portable electric water heater and faceted glass,** 1980s. Manufactured by the Vladimir Ul'ianov Mechanical Plant. This immersion electric water heater was invented by Dr Theodor Stiebel in 1924 and produced domestically in the USSR from the late 1920s. Despite being prone to fuse shortages, they remained in high demand until as late as the 1990s.

136 **Spice set**, 1960s. Prototype designed by Svetlana Mirzoyan.

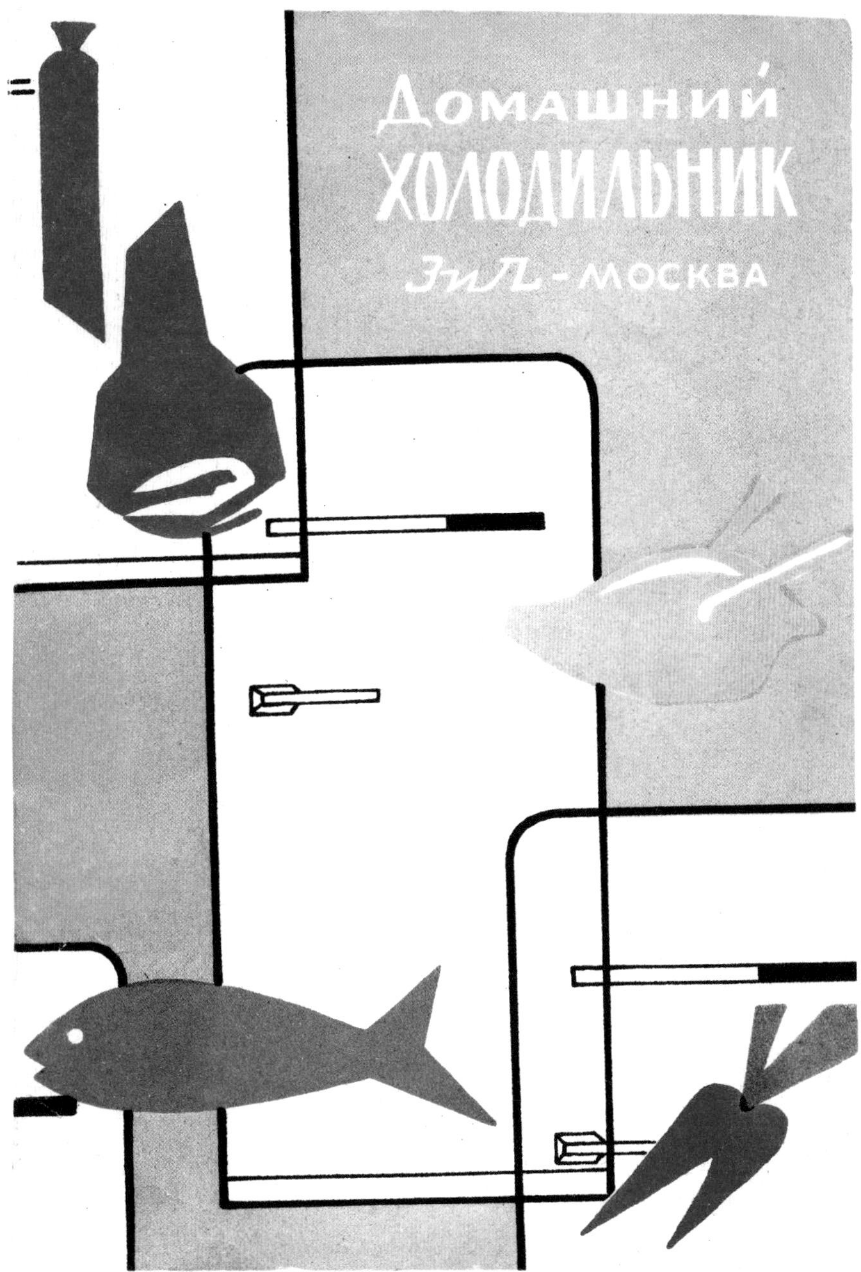

137

137 **ZIL KH 240** electric refrigerator manual, 1960–9. The Ivan Likhachov Plant, founded in 1916, is the oldest car manufacturer in Russia. It began producing electric refrigerators after World War II and its second model, the ZIL-Moskva, was the first in a series of Soviet refrigerators to be exported. During the 1970s, ZIL expanded its range with models designed by VNIITE and the famous American designer Raymond Loewy. However, most of those designs were never put into mass production. Between the 1950s and 1980s, ZIL refrigerators were considered the most stylish, reliable and prestigious in the USSR.

138

138 **Moskvich** (Muscovite) toy pedal car, 1960–73. Manufactured by the Moscow Compact Car Plant. The Moskvich was made of formed steel. It weighed about 13 kg (28.7 lbs), could reach speeds of up to 8 km/h (5 mph) and was even used in racing competitions for children aged 7 to 10. It was an expensive toy to buy but it could also be rented. Its fine finish and beautiful streamlined shape was copied from an Italian toy car, which in turn had been inspired by the American Studebaker. The next generation of Moskvich pedal cars had an original design and were similar to their lifesize counterparts produced at the Soviet plant.

139

139 **GAZ-12 ZIM** remote control car, 1955. Manufactured by the Ulyanovsk Automobile Plant.

You are following the true road, friends!

Верной дорогой идете, товарищи!

140

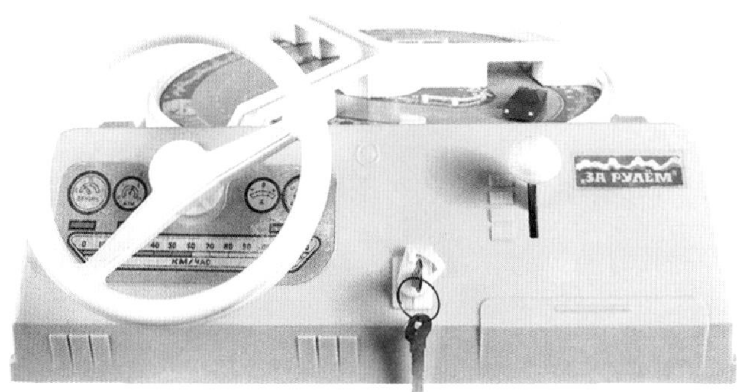

141

142

140 **Za Rulem** (Behind the Wheel) driving toy, 1970s. Manufactured by the Omsk Plant.
141 **GAZ-69** toy car, 1970s.
142 **Toy truck** with missile launcher, 1970s–80s.

143

143 **Anton, Masha and Grib Nevalyashka** roly-poly dolls, 1956–70s. Designed by the Igrushka Scientific Research Institute, manufactured by the Tambov Powder Mill. The Nevalyashka doll, which later became world famous, was originally designed for babies that have just learned to sit. It was made of bright plastic and featured a unique mechanism that made the toy return to an upright position, no matter how hard it was pushed. It also made a melodic sound when in motion. The idea behind the Nevalyashka was borrowed from the Japanese during the Russian Arts and Crafts movement in the nineteenth century.

144

145

144 **Dog** soft toy, 1950s.
145 **Fox** soft toy, 1960s.

146

146 **Toy electric stove,** 1970–80s.

147

148

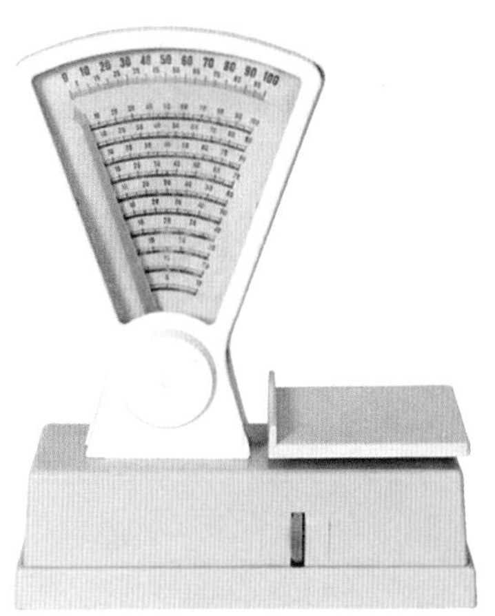

149

150

147 **Zaichik** (Rabbit) hand-operated mini-cart for children, 1970s.
148 **Toy washing machine**, 1980–90s.
149 **Toy scale**, 1980s.
150 **Toy sewing machine**, 1970s. Manufactured by the Avtopribor (Auto Appliance) Plant.

151

151 **Krokodil Gena and Cheburashka toys**, 1970–80s. Gena the Crocodile was the title character from an iconic television cartoon directed by Roman Kochanov in 1969, which itself was based on the book *Gena Crocodile and His Friends* (1966) by Eduard Uspensky. The story follows a lonely crocodile on his quest to find friends. Among others, he meets Cheburashka, a unique animal that becomes his closest companion. In 2009, an animated series called 'Cheburashka', based on the original cartoons, was created in Japan.

152

153

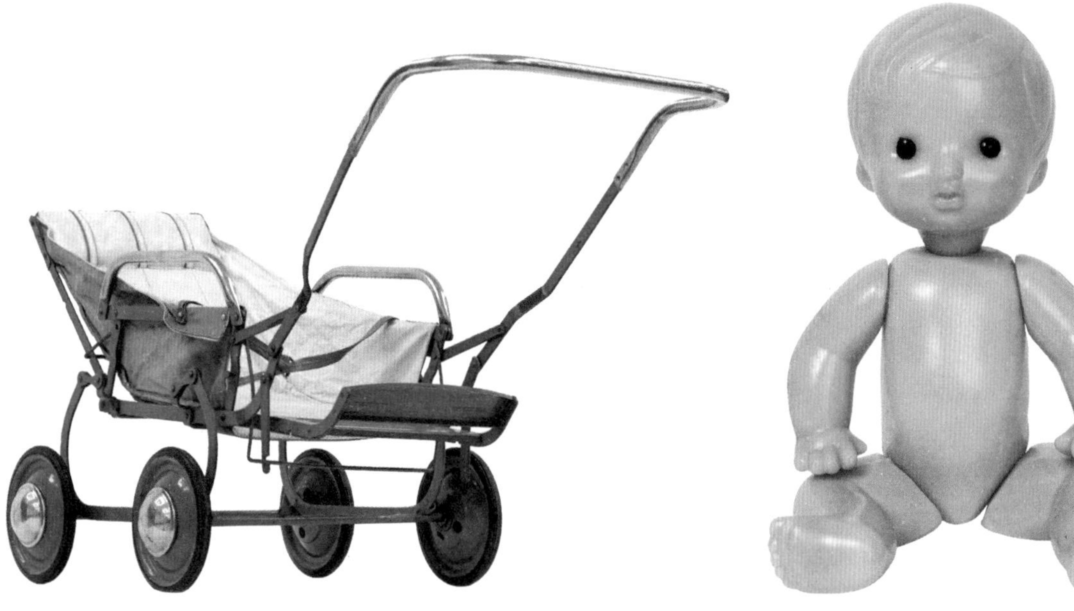

154

155

152 **Kem Bit?** (Who Do You Want To Be?) construction kit for children, 1976. Prototype designed by Alexander Lavrentiev.
153 **Theatre** construction kit for children, 1978. Prototype designed by Alexander Lavrentiev.
154 **Baby carriage**, 1960s.
155 **Golysh Pups** baby doll, 1970s. The word *pups* appeared in spoken Russian in the 1920s and referred to a cute, chubby baby. Later on, it was applied to plastic Golysh (naked) baby dolls, which were mass-produced in the Leningrad region. In the 1950s and 1960s, a pups was the most common and affordable toy. In accordance with the pedagogical recommendations of the time, the doll was made gender neutral. It was also sold naked so that children could create clothes for it themselves.

156

157

156 **Christmas Tree** plastic gift box for sweets, 1970s.
157 **Balalaika** plastic gift box for sweets, 1975.

158

159

158 **Girl in a dress** squeaky rubber doll, 1960s.
159 **Buratino** (Pinocchio) plastic toy, 1970s.
Manufactured by the Salut (Fireworks) Toy Plant.

160

160 **Kamaz** wooden toy truck, 1970s.

161

162

163

164

161 **Squirrel** rubber toy, 1970s.
162 **Squirrel** plastic toy, 1980s.
163 **Chipolino** (Little Onion) plastic toy, 1970s.
164 **Fox in a folk costume**, hand-painted gypsum prototype for rubber toy, 1970s.

Comrades, let’s do morning exercises!

Товарищи, на зарядку!

Журавль и цапля

Колобок

Марья Моревна

Никита Кожемяка

Пузырь, соломинка и лапоть

Репка

165

165 **Skazochnaya Azbuka** fairy tale book, 1969.
This book was written and illustrated in the unique style of Tatiana Mavrina, based on principles and forms found in folk art: a two-dimensional composition with silhouettes, bright colours and a non-linear narrative. A fairy tale unfolds within each letter.

166

166 **Olympic sports mosaic kit**, 1978.

167

167 **Modeling clay kit** for children, 1981.

168

168 **Sport DIY** knitted hat, 2015 (reproduction).

169

170

169 **Mari El skis**, 1960s.
170 **Hockey stick**, 1980s.

171

171 **Portable magnetic chess set**, 1980.

172

173

172 **Mechanical chess clock**, export model, 1980s. Manufactured by the Yantar Oryol Clock Factory.
173 **Portable magnetic draughts set**, 1980s.

174 **USSR athletic bag**, 1980s.

100 Citizen

CP
SR

STATE

01

С первым радостным
днем сентября
Вся страна
поздравляет тебя.
Даже солнце твердит:
–В добрый час,–
Провожая тебя
в первый класс.
БУКВАР

02

01 **Happy 1st Day of September** social awareness poster for the beginning of a new school year, 1977. Designed by Miron Lukyanov.
02 **Dream, Dare, Create!** social awareness poster, 1976.
03 **1st of September – The Day of Knowledge** social awareness poster, triptych, 1986. Designed by Miron Lukyanov.

РЯ –
НИЙ
УЧИТЬСЯ, УЧИТЬСЯ, УЧИТЬСЯ...
ПОЛИТЭКОНО
ИНФОРМАТИК
ФИЗИК
ИСТОРИЯ

03

Forward to the great goal!

Вперед, к великой цели!

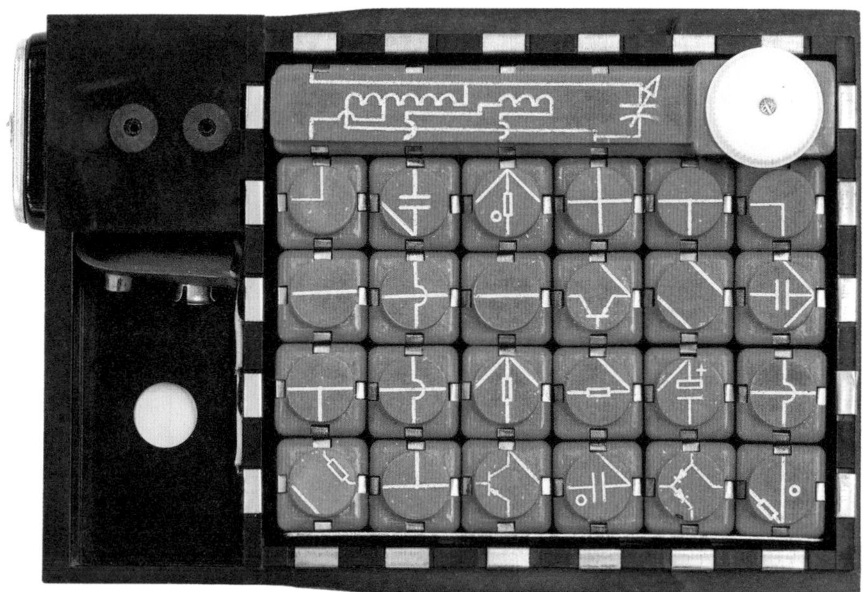

04

04 **Electronika T 802** modular radio construction kit for children, 1970s. Designed by M Felgina. The Electronika is an educational game for young radio enthusiasts. The kit consists of square modules with connectors on the outside and radio components on the inside, allowing the user to assemble different electronic devices without the use of soldering equipment. The manual describes over thirty constructions, from the simplest to more complex ones, and provides step-by-step instructions. In the 1960s and 1970s these kits became popular among teenagers, especially those who were members of the amateur radio club at their local Palace of Pioneers (a network of state educational and cultural centres for children).

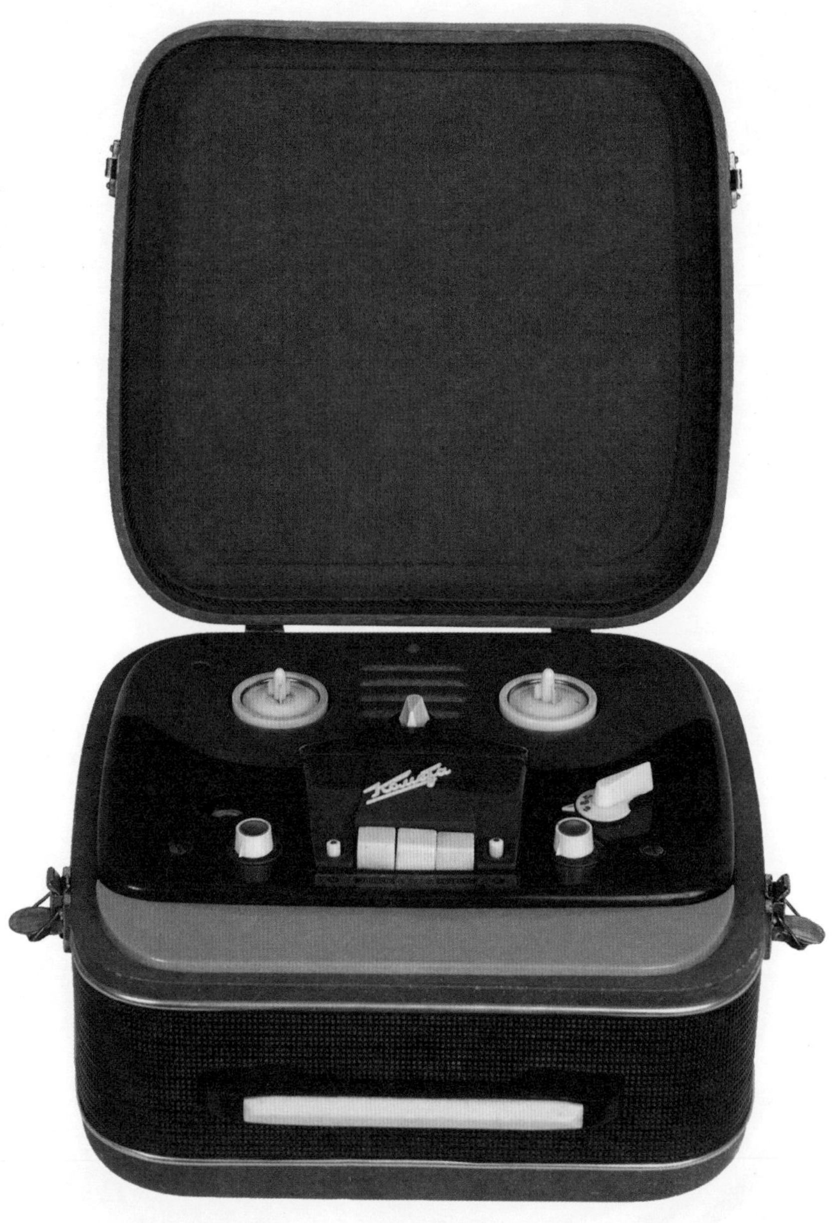

05

05 **Kometa MG-201** valve reel-to-reel tape recorder, 1965–8. Manufactured by the Tochmash Plant.

06 **Yubileyny RG-3** portable valve electrophone, 1957. Manufactured by the Leningrad Radio Equipment Factory.

07 **Elfa 6-1M** portable valve reel-to-reel tape recorder combined with electric gramophone, 1957. Manufactured by the Izhevsk Radio Manufacturing Plant.

08 **Sirius 5** electric valve radiola, 1967. Manufactured by the Izhevsk Radio Manufacturing Plant.

06

07

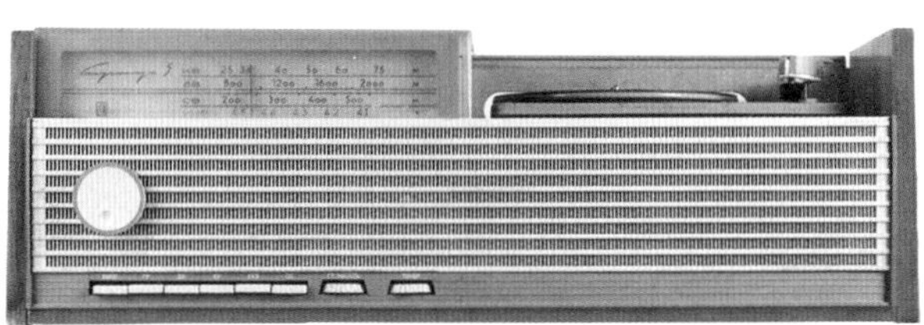

08

09

09 **Akkord** transistor electrophone, 1969–73. Manufactured by the Alexandr Popov Radio Manufacturing Plant. Electrophones were popular vinyl record players equipped with an integrated amplifier and built-in or external speakers. Most good vinyl players in the USSR, including the Vega 101, were influenced by Western examples and assembled, entirely or in part, from imported hardware components. The Akkord was designed by Adolf Irbitis (1910–83), a renowned Latvian industrial designer who worked in the field of radio equipment design for over forty years. His projects received many international accolades and in 1964, Irbitis was awarded the title of Honorary Arts Worker of Latvia.

10

10 **Rigonda-Mono** valve radiola, 1965–72. Designed by Adolf Irbitis, manufactured by the Alexandr Popov Radio Manufacturing Plant. The Rigonda-Mono was the trademark for stationary radiolas produced in the 1960s and 1970s in Riga. Its name was inspired by the imaginary island depicted in writer Vilis Lācis's novel *The Lost Homeland*, a metaphor for the Latvian capital.

11

11 **Zvezda 54** valve radio, 1954–9. Manufactured by the Kommunar Manufacturing Union and Moscow Instrument Plant. The design of the Zveszda (Star) 54 valve radio is based on an earlier French model, the Excelsior-52. It is said that when the original was presented to Lavrenty Beria, a high official in the Communist Party, he considered it so elegant that he wanted to start producing a similar model in the USSR. However, some technical alterations were required: the receiver was modified to fit the available Soviet hardware parts; the familiar red star on the front panel was added to distinguish it from the European design; and the sound quality was adapted to meet the Soviet second-class standard for audio equipment.

12

12 **Atmosfera** portable transistor radio, 1959–61. Manufactured by the Temp Leningrad Plant of Precision Electro-Mechanical Instruments, Voronezh Radio Factory and Grozny Radio Factory. Atmosfera was the first mass-produced Soviet transistor radio. Its design shows the evolution from the decorative style of the Stalinist era to the elegant, functional design of Soviet Modernism. Also available in blue and pink, it made a popular gift – this particular radio has a personalized metal plaque with a calligraphic engraving that was not a part of the original design. In 1964, this model was replaced by the Alpinist radio brand that was sold until the 1990s.

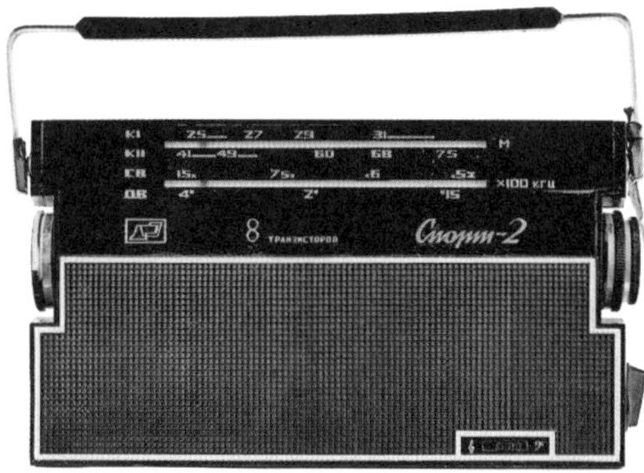

13

14

15

16

13 **Sport 2** portable transistor radio, 1966–70s. Manufactured by the Dnepropetrovsk Radio Production Plant.

14 **Selga 405** transistor radio in a leather case, 1977–85. Designed by A Sermulis, J Pelsh and D Kave, manufactured by the Alexandr Popov Radio Plant.

15 **Moskvich** wired radio, 1963–5. Manufactured by the Ritm Moscow Plant of Acoustic Aid/Hearing Devices.

16 **Avrora** wired radio, 1967–72. Manufactured by the Lianozovo Electro Mechanical Plant, Moscow.

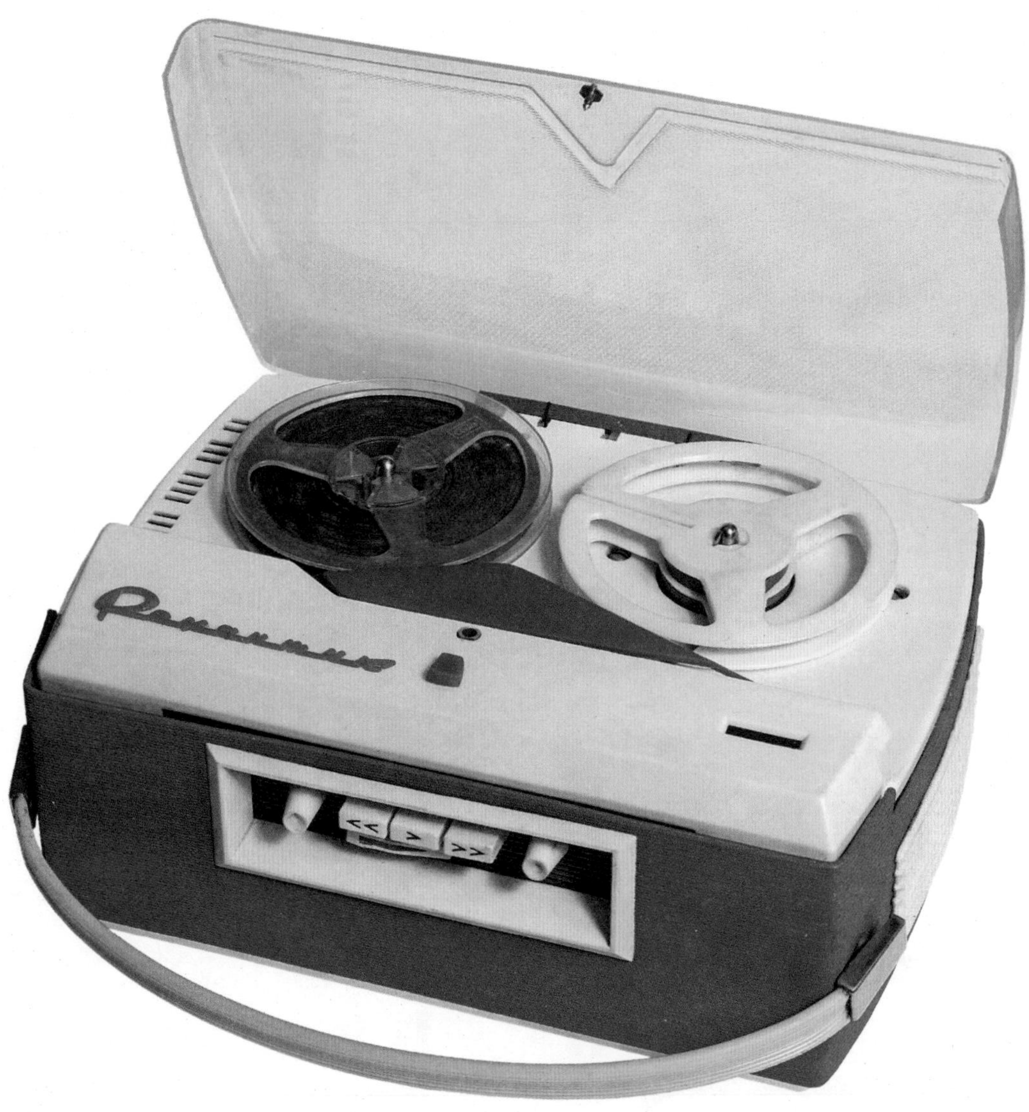

17

17 **Romantic** portable transistor reel-to-reel tape recorder, 1965–9. Manufactured by the Grigory Petrovsky Plant.

18 **Kosmos** portable radio, 1963–5. Manufactured by the Grigory Ordzhonikidze Sarapulsk Radio Plant. The first Soviet portable transistor radio, Dorozhny, was created in 1956 and resembled a small suitcase. More compact models were introduced in the late 1950s – namely Surpriz, Sputnik, Progress and Atmosfera – but technological advancements in the 1960s also enabled the miniaturization of such devices. The Kosmos prototype, developed in 1962, was small enough to fit into the palm of an adult's hand. But while it was superior to the 1963 model in both design and technical parameters, the standard box shape was chosen for production.

18

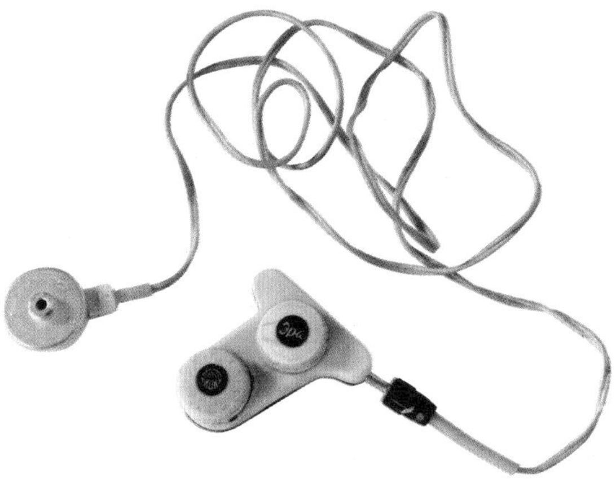

19

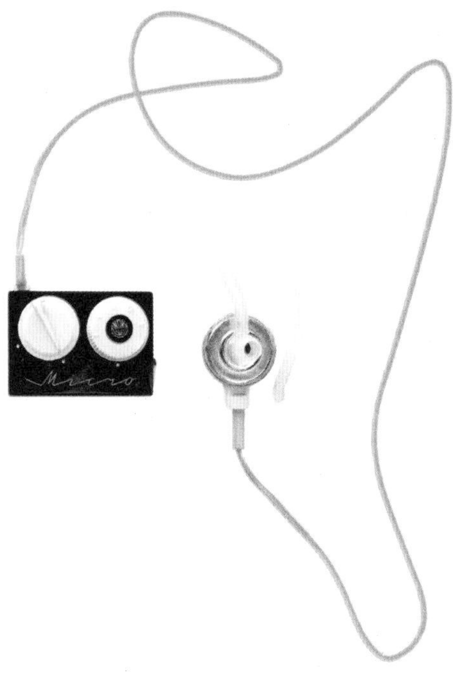

20

21

19 **Era-2M** miniature radio with headphone, 1965–9. Manufactured by the Angstrem Plant. The Era-2M, was essentially a simplified version of the Micro. Designed in the shape of an earring, it was the size of a matchbox and came equipped with an external earbud and rechargeable batteries that lasted for up to twelve hours.

20 **Micro** miniature radio with headphone, 1965–9. Manufactured by the Angstrem Plant.

21 **Spidola** transistor radio, 1960–2. Designed by Adolf Irbitis, manufactured by the Vef Radio Factory. The Spidola radio was named after the beautiful witch in the Latvian epic poem, *Lāčplēsis*. With its compact size, trapezoidal shape and stylish handle, it resembled a clutch bag. The Spidola had the capacity to receive five shortwave bands, enabling access to forbidden radio stations – partly why it was so popular.

22

Инструкция
ПОЛЬЗОВАНИЯ

23

24

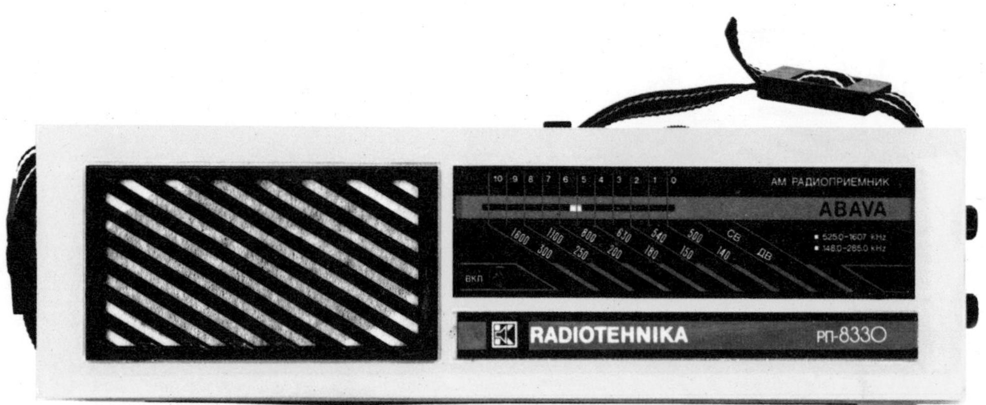

25

22 **Surpriz** (Surprise) portable transistor radio in a leather handbag case with user's manual, limited edition, 1958–9.

23 **Vef-206** portable transistor radio, 1970s. Manufactured by the Vef Radio Factory.

24 **Riga-104** portable transistor radio, 1973–8. Manufactured by the Alexandr Popov Radio Plant.

25 **Abava RP 8330** portable transistor radio, 1985–90s. Manufactured by the Vef Radio Factory, Alexandr Popov Radio Plant and Kandavas Radio Plant.

26

26 **Elektronika 324/1** portable cassette player and recorder, 1987–90s. Manufactured by the Aliot Plant. The 1980s were an era of compact cassettes when Soviet models like the Radiotekhnika, Mayak, Yauza and Vega rose in popularity. However, Japanese tape players were the most popular with Soviet citizens, especially dual-cassette recorders that allowed them to make illegal copies of hard-to-find records.

27

28

29

30

27 **Leningrad T-2** television and radio set, 1949–54. Manufactured by the Nikolai Kozitski Radio Plant. Originally manufactured in Leningrad, production of the T-2 moved to Radeberg, Germany, in 1951. It had a movable textile cover to protect the television from dust and make it appear like a radio when not in use. Its high-quality wood frame and a central decorative motif reference the Art Deco aesthetics of the Stalinist era.

28 **Start-3** television set, 1959–67. Manufactured by the Moscow Radio Engineering Plant. When compared with other affordable third-class models, the Start-3 was considered one of the best-value television sets and was exported to many ex-Socialist countries. It received twelve channels, featured an integrated radio and could be connected to a record player or reel-to-reel tape recorder.

31

29 **Chaika 4** television set, 1969–70s. Manufactured by the Vladimir Lenin Television Plant.

30 **Shilasis 405 D-1** portable television set, 1987. Manufactured by the Kaunas Radio Factory.

31 **Electronika VL100** portable television set, 1969–77. Manufactured by the Mezon Works. This model was dedicated to the 100-year anniversary of Vladimir Lenin's birth. It was available in red or blue and sold both as a ready-made set or as a DIY kit.

32

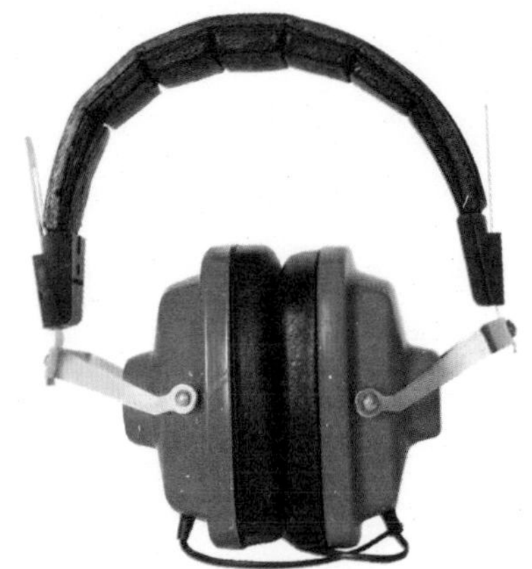

33

34

35

32 **Sfera 201** radio, 1986–91. Manufactured by the Moscow Factory of Electric Mechanisms.
33 **TDS–3** stereo headphones, 1977–80s. Manufactured by the Ryazan Radio Manufacturing Plant
34 – 35 **Electronika TS-401 M** portable television set, 1984. Manufactured by the Moscow Electric Lamp Plant.
36 **Electronika 591** portable colour reel-to-reel video tape recorder, 1982. Manufactured by the Kompleks Nizhny Novgorod Manufacturing Union.

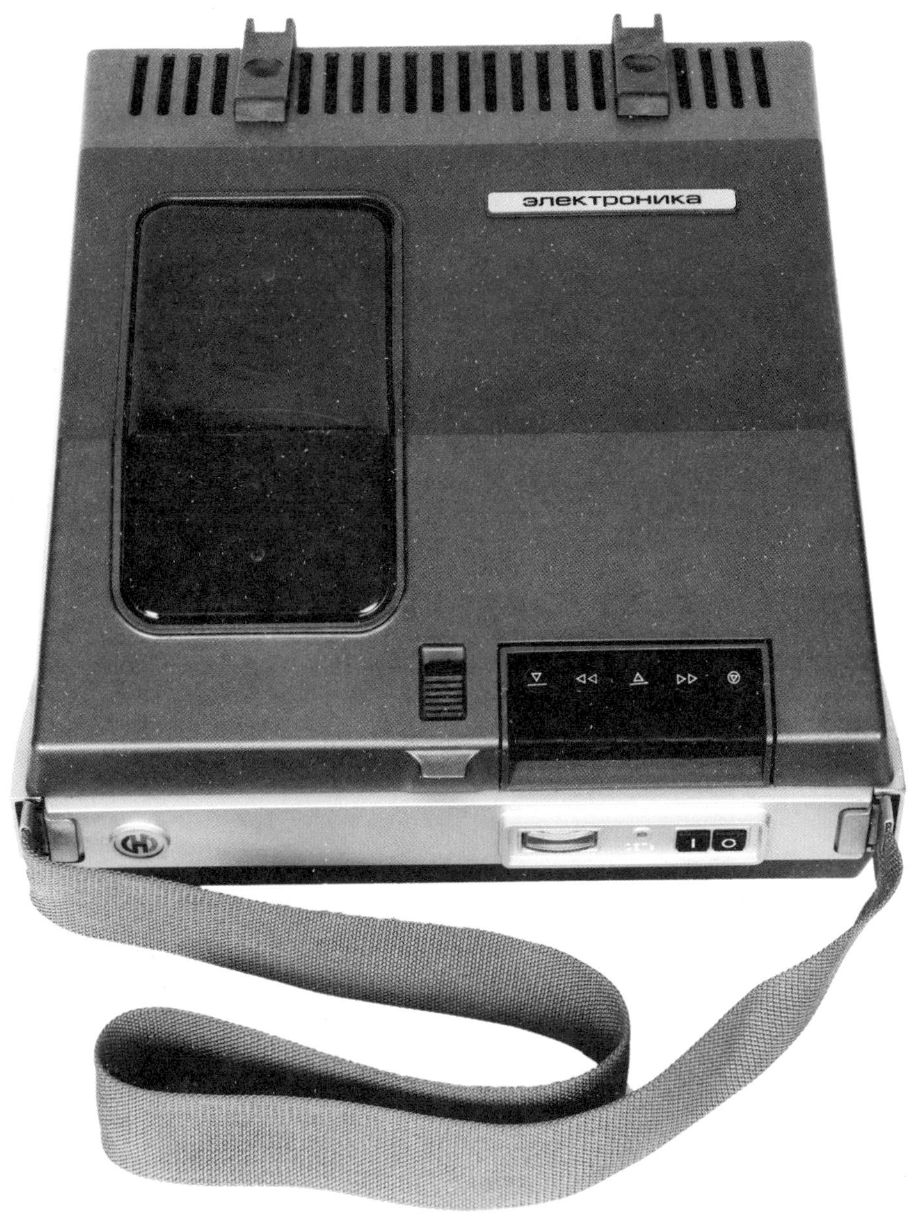

36

37 **Novie Tovari** (New Goods) magazine, No. 1, 1972.
38 **Novie Tovari** (New Goods) magazine, No. 11, 1961. *Novie Tovari* was a monthly publication featuring what the USSR Ministry of Commerce considered the best examples of consumer goods. It showcased the latest innovations in household appliances, electronic engineering, cosmetics, clothes, shoes, vehicles and toys. It featured articles by ministry officials as well as industrial and commercial workers that discussed mass production, design and product quality. However, far from being a reflection of Soviet daily life, *Novie Tovari* was mainly focused on touting the industry's recent achievements – in reality, most of the featured goods were either too expensive or rarely available in Soviet shops.

37

Новые 1 1972
товары

Всесоюзный Павильон лучших образцов
Новые
ТОВАРЫ
1961
11
Информационный бюллетень

ХУДОЖЕСТВЕННЫЙ ФИЛЬМ
дождливое воскресенье
Автор сценария ЖУЖА ПОНГРАЦ
Режиссер МАРТОН КЕЛЕТИ
Оператор ТИБОР ВАДЬОЦКИ
Художник БЕЛА ЗАЙХАН
Композитор САБОЛЬЧ ФЕНЕШ
Роли исполняют:
Дёнди ПОЛОНИ, Тери ТОРДАИ,
Илона БЕРЕШ, Ютка ХАЛАС,
Антал ПАГЕР и др.
ПРОИЗВОДСТВО
КИНОСТУДИИ „ГУННИЯ". ВЕНГРИЯ
Фильм дублирован Центральной
студией киноактера „МОСФИЛЬМ"

39

40

41

39 **Dozhdlivoe Voskresen'e** (Rainy Sunday) movie poster, 1963. Designed by Miron Lukyanov.

40 **Tabletop telephone** with quality mark, 1970s. As the use of rotary telephones became more widespread, organizations instead moved to an internal telephone network. Telephones without a rotary dial became the new status symbol, providing a direct line of communication to Party bosses and state officals.

41 **Kremlovskaya Vertushka STA-2** Kremlin telephone, 1970s. When the Kremlin's first switchboard was installed, users of the regular telephone network could only place calls via an operator. Vertushka users, however, could make direct calls using a rotary dial. Adorned with the USSR state emblem, these official devices were secure from phone-tapping due to their shielded components and graphite film interior lining.

We grow under the sun of our country.

Мы растем под солнцем нашей страны.

42 

43 

42 **Bez Strakha I Upreka** (Without Fear and Beyond Reproach) movie poster, 1962. Designed by Miron Lukyanov, directed by Aleksander Mitta.

43 **Vesennie Khlopoti** (Spring Cares) movie poster, 1964. Designed by Miron Lukyanov, directed by Jan Fried and Maksimas Rufas.

44 **Afera V Kazino** (The Casino Affair) movie poster, 1957. Designed by Miron Lukyanov, directed by Arthur Pohl.

45 **Drug Moi, Kol'ka!** (My Friend, Kolka!) movie poster, 1961. Designed by Miron Lukyanov, directed by Aleksei Saltykov and Aleksander Mitta.

ХУДОЖЕСТВЕННЫЙ ФИЛЬМ
Автор сценария и режиссер Артур ПОЛЬ
Оператор Иоахим ХАССЛЕР
Композитор Мартин БЁТТХЕР
Роли исполняют:
Гертруд КЮКЕЛЬМАН, Ян ХЕНДРИКС,
Рудольф ФОРСТЕР, Петер ПАЗЕТТИ,
Свен ЛИНДБЕРГ, Вилли А. КЛЕЙНАУ
ПРОИЗВОДСТВО КИНОСТУДИИ ДЕФА
(ГДР), „А. Б. ПАНДОРА ФИЛЬМ“ (ШВЕЦИЯ)
Фильм дублирован киностудией
„Союзмультфильм“
АФЕРА в КАЗИНО
Заказ 1242
Тираж 86 000

45

ХУДОЖЕСТВЕННЫЙ ФИЛЬМ
Постановка АЛЕКСЕЯ САЛТЫКОВА, АЛЕКСАНДРА МИТТЫ
ДРУГ МОЙ, КОЛЬКА!
Сценарий АЛЕКСАНДРА ХМЕЛИКА
при участии С. ЕРМОЛИНСКОГО
ПРОИЗВОДСТВО
ТВОРЧЕСКОГО ОБЪЕДИНЕНИЯ ДЕТСКИХ ФИЛЬМОВ.
КИНОСТУДИЯ „МОСФИЛЬМ“

46

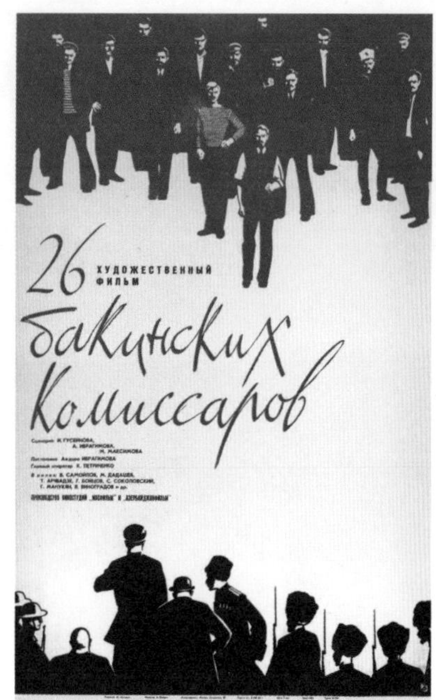

47

48

49

46 **Chistye Prudy** (Clear Ponds) movie poster, 1965. Designed by Miron Lukyanov, directed by Alexey Sakharov.

47 **26 Bakinskikh Komissarov** (26 Baku Commissars) movie poster, 1966. Designed by Miron Lukyanov, directed by Azhdar Ibragimov.

48 **Vrema, Vpered!** (Time, Forward!) movie poster, 1965. Designed by Miron Lukyanov, directed by Sofiya Milkina and Mikhail Shveytser.

49 **Chernaya Chaika** (Black Seagull) movie poster, 1962. Designed by Miron Lukyanov, directed by Grigori Koltunov.

50

51

52

53

50 **Chernie Ochki** (Black Sunglasses) movie poster, 1964. Designed by Miron Lukyanov, directed by Houssam El-Din Mustafa.

51 **Molodo-Zeleno** (Young and Green) movie poster, 1962. Designed by Miron Lukyanov, directed by Konstantin Voinov.

52 **Kogo My Bolshe Lyubim** (Who Do We Love More) movie poster, 1964. Designed by Miron Lukyanov, directed by Zeinab Kazimova, Arif Babaev and Gasan Seidbeili.

53 **Vecherinka** (The Party) movie poster, 1963. Designed by Miron Lukyanov, directed by Joze Babic.

54

ВЕНГЕРСКИЙ ХУДОЖЕСТВЕННЫЙ ФИЛЬМ
с СУББОТЫ
Автор сценария ЗОЛТАН ХЕГЕДЮШ
Режиссер ДЬЮЛА МЕСАРОШ
Оператор ЯНОШ ТОТ
Роли исполняют:
МАРИАНА МООР, ЕВА ВАШ,
ИРЕН ШЮТЭ, МАГДА ГАБИ,
ЙОЖЕФ ЛАНГ, ЖИГМОНД ФЮЛЭП
и др.
Производство
киностудии „Гунния", 1959 г.
Фильм дублирован на киностудии
им. М. Горького
до
ПОНЕДЕЛЬНИКА

55

ХУДОЖЕСТВЕННЫЙ
ФИЛЬМ
Я,
БАБУШКА,
ИЛИКО
И
ИЛЛАРИОН
(По одноименному рассказу Н. ДУМБАДЗЕ)
Авторы сценария: Нодар ДУМБАДЗЕ, Тенгиз АБУЛАДЗЕ
Режиссер-постановщик Тенгиз АБУЛАДЗЕ
Главный оператор Георгий КАЛАТОЗИШВИЛИ
Художники: Гиви ГИГАУРИ, Кахи ХУЦИШВИЛИ
Композиторы: Арчил КАРЕСЕЛИДЗЕ, Нугзар ВАЦАДЗЕ
Звукооператор Рафаил КОЗЕЛИ
Роли исполняют: Зураб ОРДЖОНИКИДЗЕ, Сесиля ТАКАИШВИЛИ, Александр ЖОРЖОЛИАНИ, Григорий ТКАБЛАДЗЕ и др.
ПРОИЗВОДСТВО КИНОСТУДИИ „ГРУЗИЯ-ФИЛЬМ"
Фильм дублирован на киностудии им. М. Горького

56

54 **Vremya Otdykha S Subboty Do Ponedelnika** (Leisure Time from Saturday to Monday) movie poster, 1959. Designed by Miron Lukyanov, directed by Dula Mesarosh.

55 **Ya, Babushka, Iliko I Illarion** (Me, Grandmother, Iliko and Illarion) movie poster, 1963. Designed by Miron Lukyanov, directed by Tengiz Abuladze. In this dynamic poster design, the film's main characters are depicted in the upper right corner, positioned as if walking into the frame. In the bottom left corner the tail end of a dog is seen running out of view, creating a sense of movement. This composition draws the viewer's attention to the typograpic arrangement, which is generously spaced, creating a light and airy feel. The type's slightly scuffed texture hints at the passage of time and evokes a sense of craftsmanship.

57

56 **Waiting for Instructions from the Centre** poster, 1989. This poster, by the famous Soviet political cartoonist Boris Yefimov, satirizes the notion of a local manager who ignores the requests and initiatives of individuals piling up beneath his desk and only waits for instructions from his boss.

57 **Tabletop flip calendar**, 1950s. Manufactured by Gosznak Leningrad Mint Factory.

58

58 **Beregis Avtomobilya** (Beware of the Car) original gouache drawing for movie poster, 1960s. Designed by Miron Lukyanov, directed by Eldar Ryazano.

59

59 **Kalashnikov toy gun**, 1960s.

КИНОКОМЕДИЯ
МАРШРУТ
Автор сценария МАТИАШ ЧИЗМАРЕК
Режиссер ДЬЁРДЬ ПАЛАШТИ
Оператор МИКЛОШ ГЕРЦЕНИК
Художник МЕЛИНДА ВАШАРИ
Композитор ФЕРЕНЦ ЛОВАШ
Художник М. Лукьянов
Редактор З. Померанцева
«Рекламфильм»,

ли исполняют: ЙОЖЕФ СЕНДРЭ,
НАИ, ИМРЕ РАДАИ, ХИЛЬДА ГОББИ,
Ш ПАНДИ, ЛАСЛО МАРКУШ,
КАЛЛАИ, ШАНДОР ПЕТИ и др.

ПРОИЗВОДСТВО
КИНОСТУДИИ „ГУННИЯ". ВЕНГРИЯ
Фильм дублирован на киностудии им. М. Горького

дп. в печ. 28.XII—62 г. Цена 10 шт.—37 коп. Заказ 1637 Тираж 82 000

61

60 **Marshrut 99** (Route 99) movie poster, 1961. Designed by Miron Lukyanov, directed by Palásthy György.

61 **Posle Svadbi** (After the Wedding) movie poster, 1962. Designed by Miron Lukyanov, directed by Mikhail Ershov.

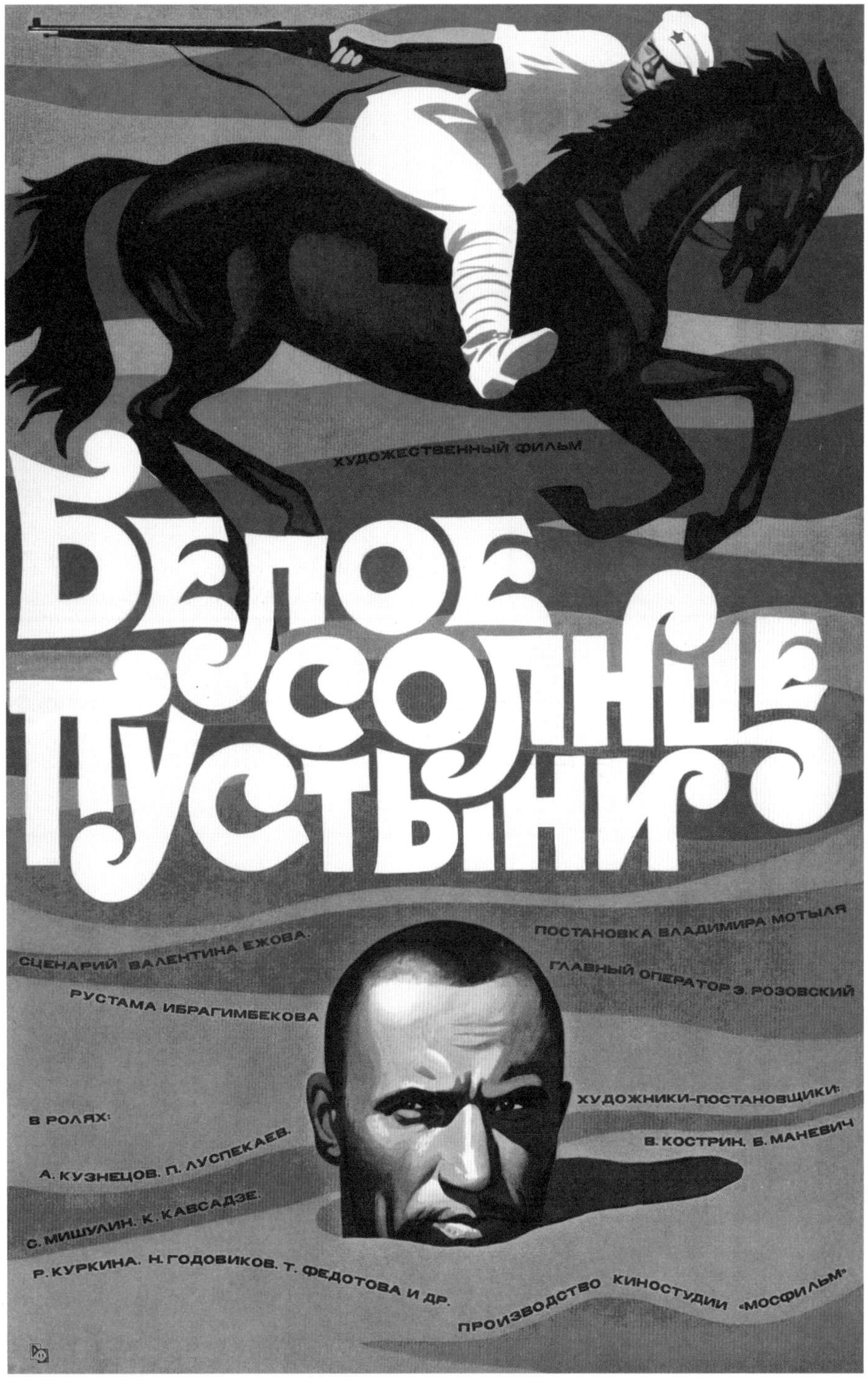

62

62 **Beloe Solntse Pustyni** (White Sun of the Desert) movie poster, 1970. Designed by Miron Lukyanov, directed by Vladimir Motyl. The unique lettering on this movie poster makes it an essential part of the artistic statement; its boldly curving edges evocative of sand billowing behind the hooves of the horse. The upper part of the artwork is full of movement and dynamism and the image of an armed rider, heroically fighting off his enemies with a gun, highlights the influence of America's popular western movie genre. In contrast, the lower part features an ominous image of a man's head sticking out of the sand. His severe expression commands the viewers' attention, building interest in his fate. The poster uses a saturated southern palette – yellow and orange contrast with deep shades of lilac – to create a sense of exhausting heat.

63

64

65

63 **Pedestrian, Self-Discipline Will Guarantee Your Safety!** social awareness poster, 1974. Designed by Miron Lukyanov.

64 **Moskvich C-1** fully functional lifesize car model, 1975. Manufactured by the Leninist Communist Youth Union Automobile Plant. This model had the unofficial title of Krokodil Gena because of its long horizontal proportions and bright-green colour. The car had a dynamic fastback body style and sedan trunk. Despite its innovate engineering, only three cars were ever built.

65 **Moskvich 408** right-hand drive model for export, 1964–75. Designed by B Ivanov. The Moskvich 408 was the first fuel-efficient car produced by the Moscow Compact Car Plant. This small family car model had a completely new body design and was so popular that it was manufactured for export.

Береги
АВТОМОБ
Сценарий Э. БРАГИНСКОГО, Э. РЯЗАНОВА
Постановка Эльдара РЯЗАНОВА
Операторы: А. МУКАСЕЙ, В. НАХАБЦЕВ
Художники: Б. НЕМЕЧЕК, Л. СЕМЕНОВ
Композитор А. ПЕТРОВ
Звукооператор В. ПОПОВ
В главных ролях:
ИННОКЕНТИЙ СМОКТУНОВСКИЙ
И ОЛЕГ ЕФРЕМОВ
В фильме снимались: Л. ДОБРЖАНС
О. АРОСЕВА, А. МИРОНОВ, А. ПАПА
Т. ГАВРИЛОВА, Г. ЖЖЕНОВ, Е. ЕВСТИ
С. КУЛАГИН, В. РАНДУНСКАЯ
ПРОИЗВОДСТВО КИНОСТУДИИ «МОСФИЛЬ

66

КИНОКОМЕДИЯ
СЬ
ИЯ

67

66 **Beregis Avtomobilya (Beware of the Car)** movie poster, 1966. Designed by Anatoly Yevseev and Pavel Zolotarevsky. The Volga rose to fame in the popular comedy drama *Beware of the Car*, directed by Eldar Ryazanov. The film's protagonist, Yuri Detochkin, is a Soviet Robin Hood who steals Volgas belonging to corrupt officials, profiteers and thieves, and anonymously transfers the profits to the accounts of various orphanages. The car thus came to symbolize its owner's status and sometimes even implied that their income came from illegal sources. For the poster design, Yevseev and Zolotarevsky created a triptych merging several camera angles to produce a dynamic and symbolic composition in the style of renowned movie posters from the 1920s and 1930s by the Stenberg brothers (Vladimir and Georgii).

68

67 – 68 **Volga GAZ-M21**, 1956–70. Manufactured by the Gorky Automobile Plant. The Volga is one of the Soviet automotive industry's iconic symbols. Its elegant body and exceptionally smooth ride on rough roads (and even off-road) led the Western press to call it a tank in a tailcoat. Compared to mass-produced European cars, the Volga was both affordable and spacious, but it was also quite stylish. In the spirit of American cruisers, its design was partially based on those of foreign manufacturers such as Ford, Opel and Chevrolet, but the resulting model has a completely original design. In 1958, the Volga was awarded a gold medal at the Brussels World's Fair.

With great labour we will fulfil the plan.

Выполним план великих работ.

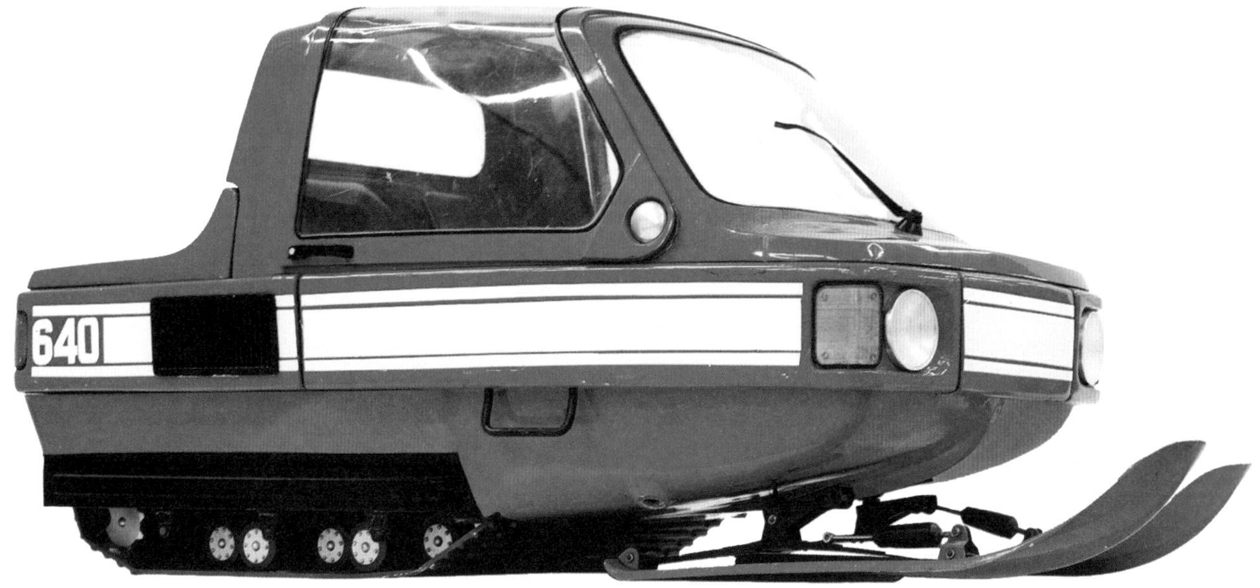

69

69 **Scale model for an experimental closed-cabin snowmobile**, 1980s. Designed by Nikolai Kaptelin and Alexey Popov (VNIITE). One area of interest for VNIITE was in the development of off-road winter passenger vehicles for professional, sport, tourist and recreational use. The main goal of the project was to increase comfort, speed and safety for the user. This was the first Soviet snowmobile to feature a closed-cabin and was therefore both warm and soundproof. It was also the first time that fibreglass was proposed to replace steel during production. This would offer resistance from the corrosion inflicted by snow and tree branches. Unfortunately, the project did not progress beyond the proposal stage.

70

70 **Three-wheel truck** scale model prototype, 1980s.
Designed by VNIITE.

71

72

73

71 **Forklift truck** scale model prototype, 1987.
Designed by Igor Levit (VNIITE).

72 **Heavy goods vehicle** scale model prototype, 1980s.
Designed by VNIITE.

73 **Combine harvester** scale model prototype, 1980s.
Designed by VNIITE.

74

74 **Hydro-copying machine** design and ergonomic research image, commissioned by Utita, Italy, 1975. Designed by Alexander Grashin, Lev Kuz'michev, J Fainleib and V Prokhorenko, among other VNIITE members.

75

75 **Hydro-copying machine** commissioned by Utita, Italy, 1975. Designed by Alexander Grashin, Lev Kuz'michev, J Fainleib and V Prokhorenko, among other VNIITE members.

76

76 **Hydro-copying machine** design and ergonomic research image, commissioned by Utita, Italy, 1975. Designed by Alexander Grashin, Lev Kuz'michev, J Fainleib and V Prokhorenko, among other VNIITE members.

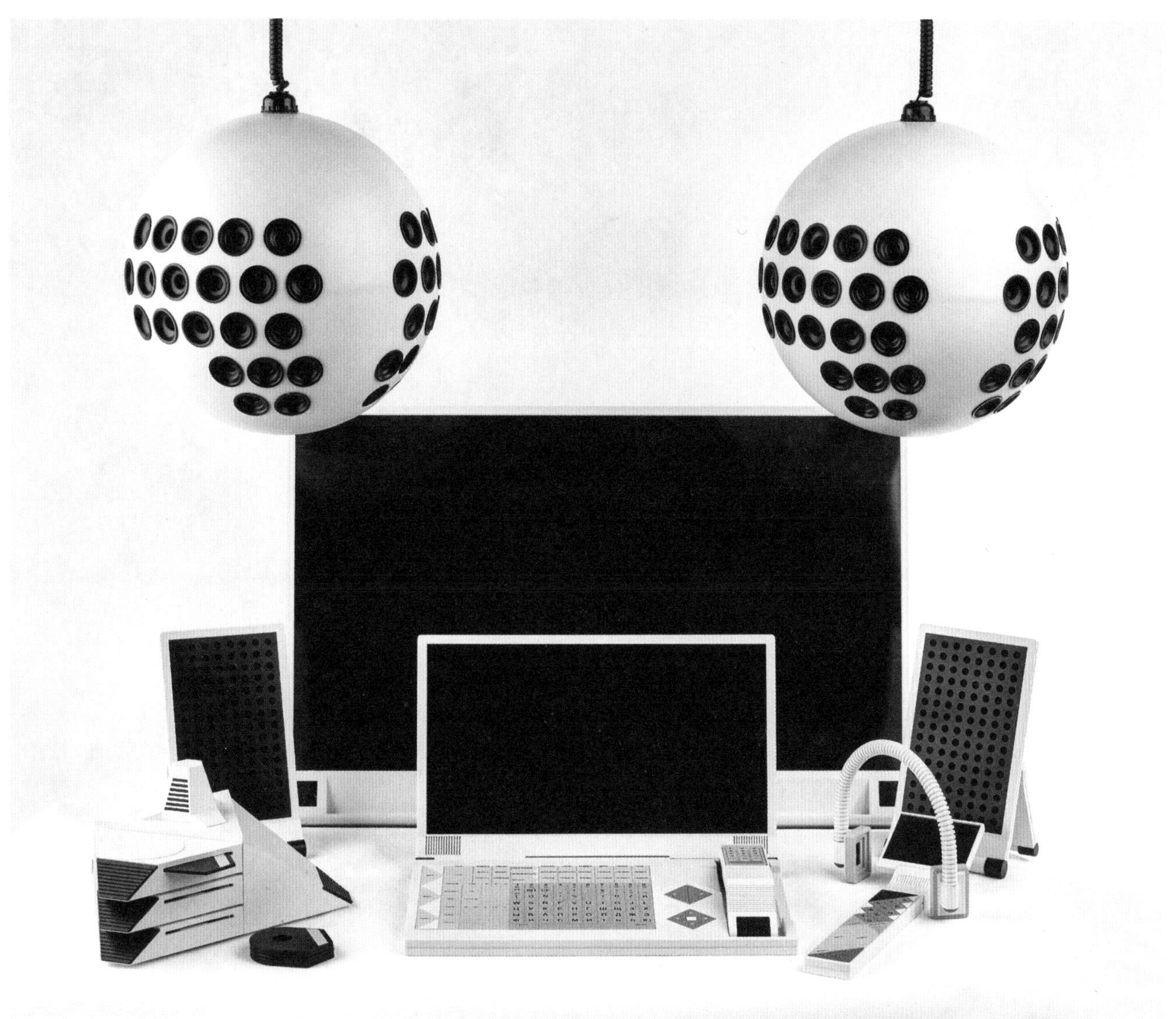

77

77 **Sphinx** super-functional integrated communicative system, 1986. Designed by Dmitry Azrikan, Igor Lisenko, Alexey Kolotushkin, Marina Mikheeva, Elena Ruzova and Maria Kolotushkina (VNIITE), published in *Technical Aesthetics* magazine, No. 9, 1987. This 'smart house' project included spherical loudspeakers, monitors, headphones, remote control with removable touch display, floppy disk storage and a processor with three memory-management units, among many other features. In designing a model for a combined home television and radio centre for the year 2000, the Sphinx creators actually managed to foresee many trends of the new millenium.

78

79

78 – 79 **Tabletop telephones**, 1980s. Prototypes designed by VNIITE.

80 

81 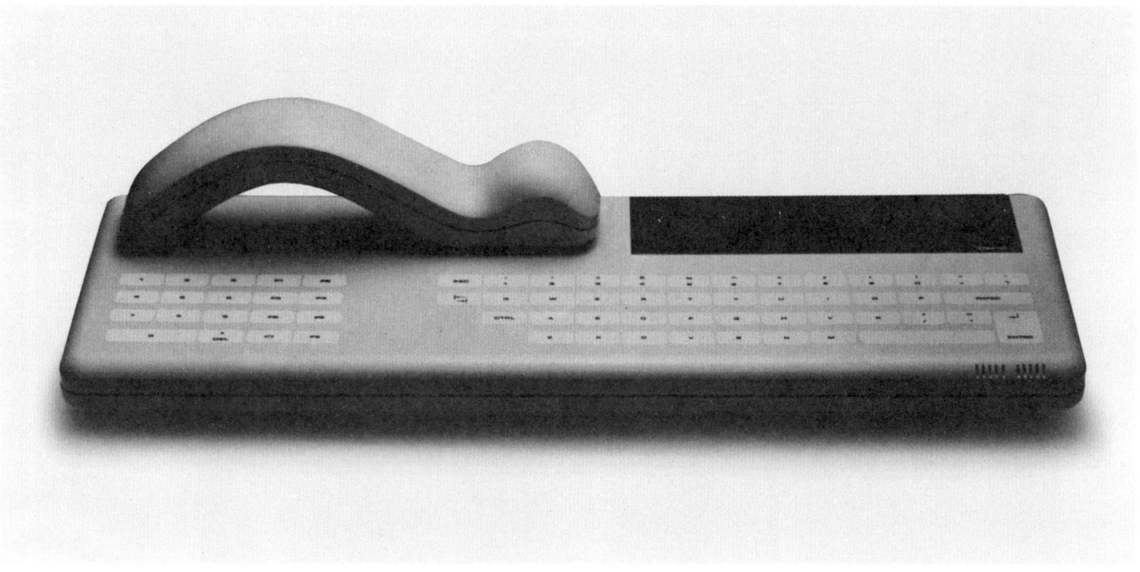

80 **Cordless telephone**, 1989. Prototype designed by Andrey Taube (VNIITE).
81 **Tabletop telephone**, 1980s. Prototype designed by VNIITE.

82–83 **Designers Society of the USSR** promotional brochure published for the union's first congress, 1986. The Designers Society of the USSR, established in 1986 through the efforts of Yuri Soloviev, made it possible for Soviet designers to establish private studios and legitimized the notion of the word 'design' in the Russian language.

СОЮЗ ДИЗАЙНЕРОВ
СССР
THE USSR
DESIGNERS' SOCIETY

83

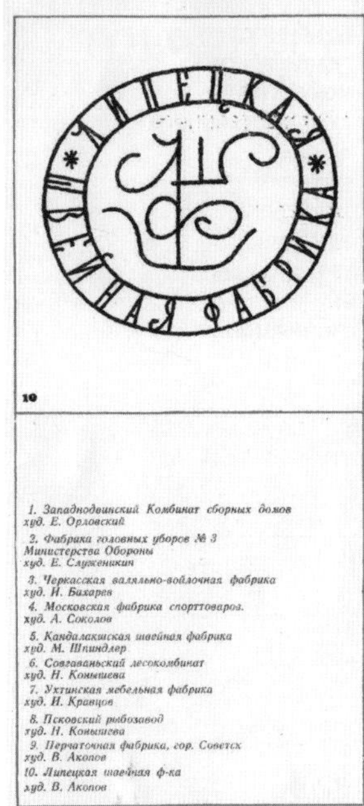

84

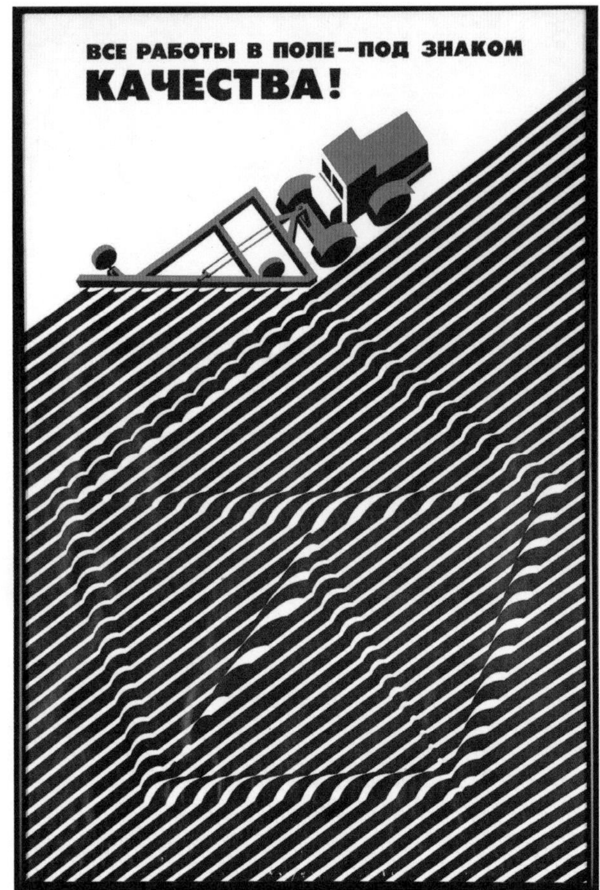

85

86

84 **Promotional brochure** for the Workshop of Artists of Applied and Industrial Graphics, 1960s.

85 **All Fieldwork Done Under the Quality Mark!** social awareness poster, 1970s. This poster was designed by Miron Lukyanov using Op Art graphic techniques popular in the 1970s and incorporates the famous quality mark logo created by prominent typeface designer Vladimir Lazurskiy. The mark's shape echoes the form of the USSR pennant that was placed on the moon during the Lunar 2 landing in 1959. Within this sits a five-pointed star, which, when rotated 90 degrees, also appears to resemble the letter K, the first letter in *kachestvo*, the Russian word for quality.

86 **Crown cap** with quality mark, 1960–80s. Since there was no competition for consumers in the Soviet Union's planned economy, it was up to the state to

87

88

stimulate product improvement. To do this, the government introduced a certification system that would rate products as either top, first or second quality. Top category items were awarded a quality mark while decertified items were withdrawn from production.

87 **AT-100s** soda water vending machine, 1970–80s. Manufactured at the Kharkov, Kiev and Perovsk Mechanical Engineering Plants.

88 **Collapsible cup for liquids**, 1980s. These cheap, reusable, collapsible cups were part of the Soviet sustainable way of life. In the USSR, beer, wine, and non-alcoholic drinks were sold on the streets in vending machines that came equipped with a communal drinking glass. With no disposable alternative, collapsible cups were a much-needed solution to a potentially unpleasant situation.

89

89 **Na Lednike Fedchenko** (On Fedchenko Glacier) movie poster, 1961. Designed by Miron Lukyanov.

90 **Vkus Svezhego Vetra** (The Feel of Fresh Wind) movie poster, 1963. Designed by Miron Lukyanov.

91 **Get Ready!** social awareness poster, 1965. Designed by Miron Lukyanov and Vasily Ostrovskiy.

90

91

92

93

92 **Toward New Records!** social awareness poster, 1971. Designed by Miron Lukyanov.

93 **Train Your Muscles, Breath and Body for the Art of War** social awareness poster, 1972. Designed by Miron Lukyanov.

94 **Let's Be Polite To Each Other!** social awareness poster, 1974. Designed by Miron Lukyanov.

95 **Young People, Go to the Textile Industry!** social awareness poster, 1970s. Designed by Miron Lukyanov.

94

БУДЕМ ВЗАИМНО ВЕЖЛИВЫ!

95

WORLD

01

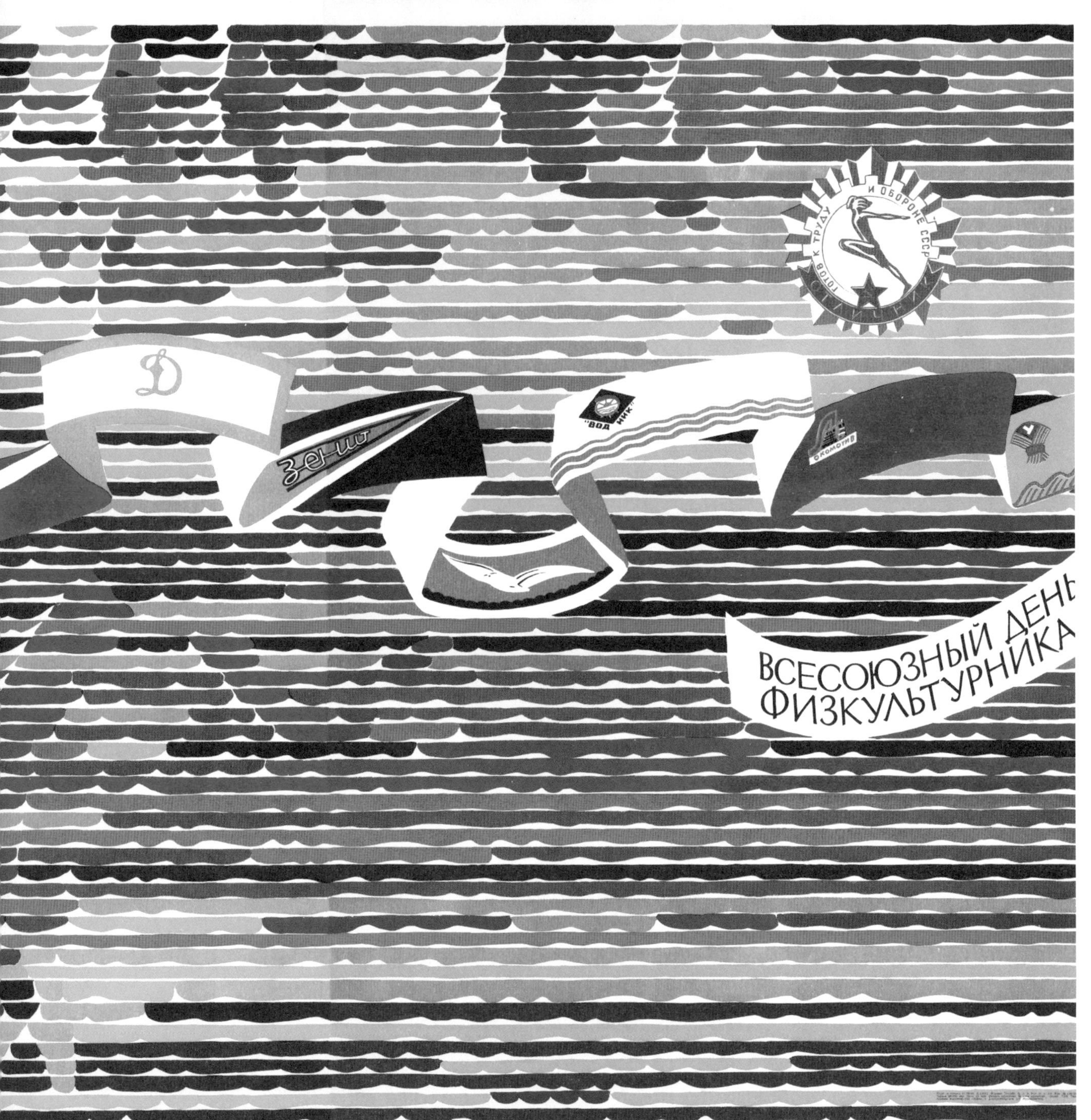
И ОБОРОНЕ СССР
ВСЕСОЮЗНЫЙ ДЕНЬ
ФИЗКУЛЬТУРНИКА

02

01 **Millions at the Starting Line** Olympic Games promotional poster, 1981. Designed by Miron Lukyanov.

02 **Athletic uniform for the Torch Relay**, 1980. Designed and manufactured by Mizuno, Japan. The uniform consisted of a sleeveless shirt, shorts, a headband and sneakers.

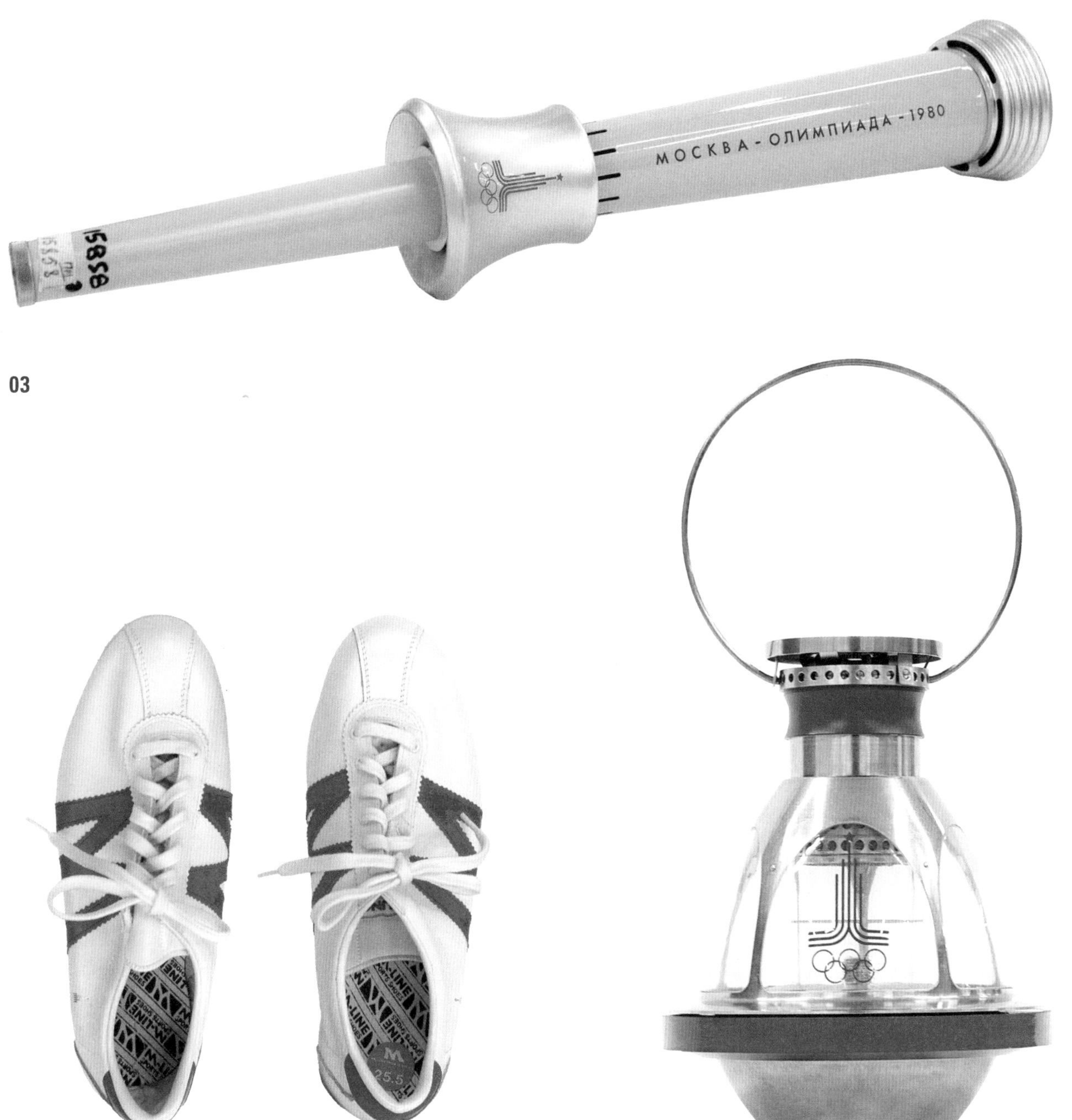

03

04

05

03 **Olympic Torch**, 1980. Designed by students of the Vera Mukhina Arts and Crafts School, manufactured by the Jakov Klimov Plant.

04 **Athletic sneakers for the Torch Relay**, 1980. Designed and manufactured by Mizuno, Japan.

05 **Reserve lamp for the Olympic Flame**, 1980. Manufactured by the Jakov Klimov Plant. The Japanese company Mizuno, official supplier of uniforms for the Olympic Torch Relay, was initially commissioned to design the torch. However, six months before the opening of the games, its proposal was rejected. Under the supervision of Boris Tuchin, a new design was created by students of the Vera Mukhina Arts and Crafts School in Leningrad. Each of the 6,200 torches contained a canister of liquefied gas and an olive oil-impregnated fuse to give the flame a pink tinge.

06

06 **Soap packaging** with Misha the Bear Olympic mascot, 1980. Manufactured by the Svoboda Cosmetic Factory.

07 **Svema magnetic tape packaging** with Misha the Bear Olympic mascot, 1980. Manufactured by the Svema Manufacturing Group.

08 **Thermos flask** with Misha the Bear Olympic mascot, 1980.

07

08

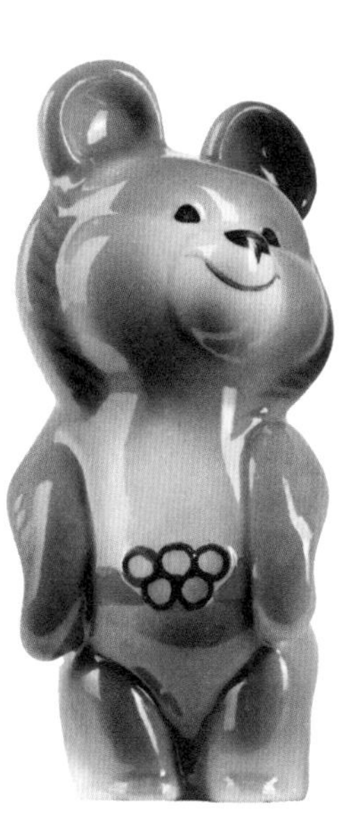

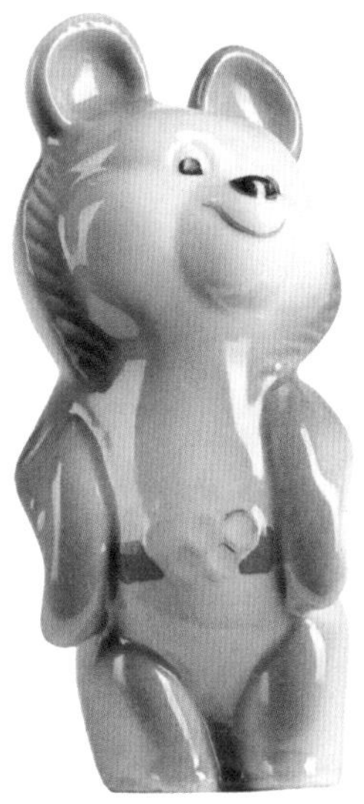

09

09 **Olympic Games mascot figurines**, 1980s. Manufactured by the Dulevo Porcelain Factory. A bear was chosen as the Olympic mascot in a poll conducted by the popular television nature programme 'V Mire Zhivotnikh' ('In the Animal World'). The Olympic Committee then held a competition to decide on a suitable design and requested submissions from well-known Soviet illustrators. Talented children's book illustrator Victor Chizhikov won with his strong but friendly and approachable little bear. The original character was drawn in watercolour, which gave it a soft and furry appearance. This was the first time the Olympic mascot was represented full-face rather than in profile, which helped the bear to build a strong emotional connection with visitors to the games.

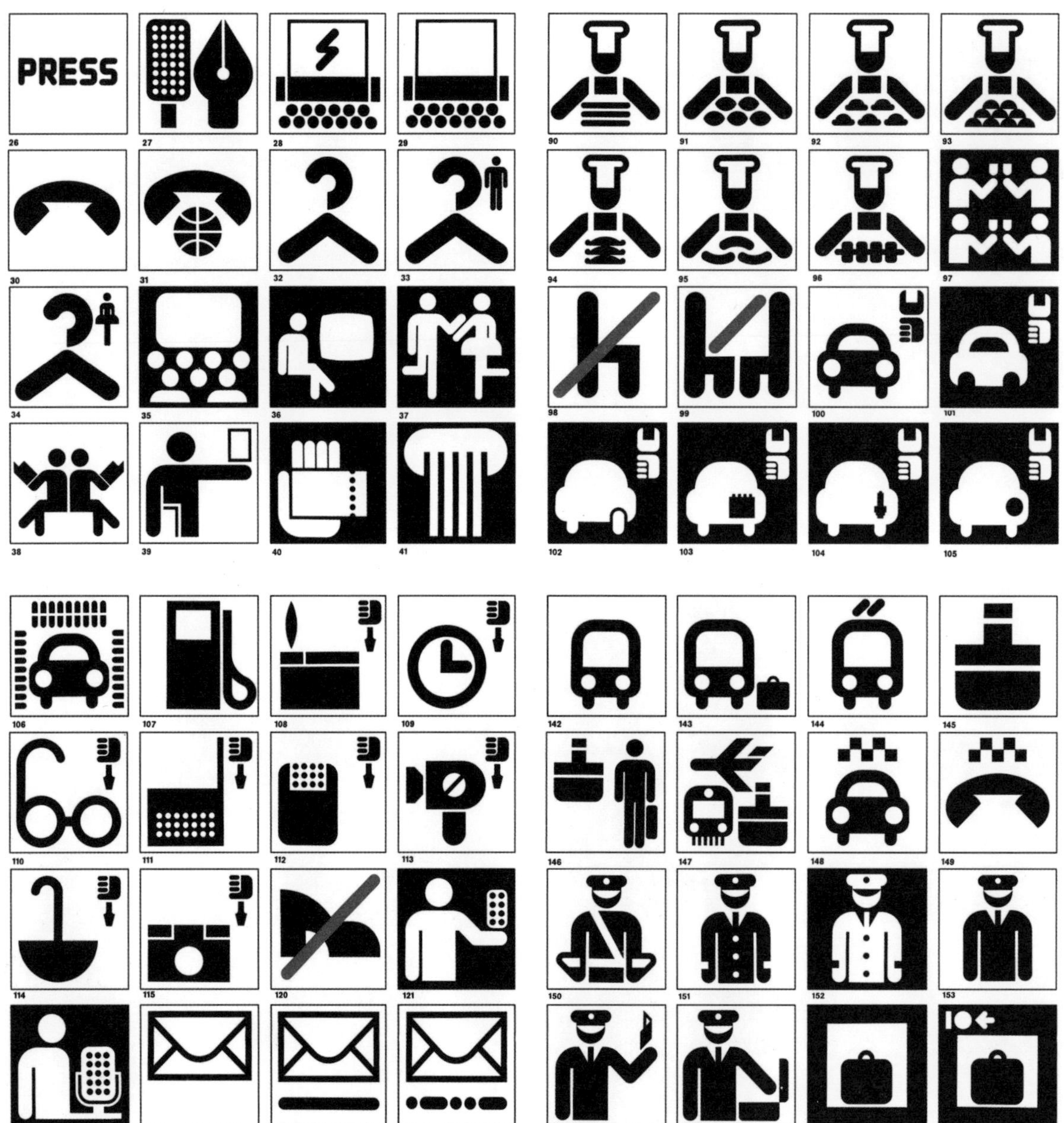

10

10 **Pictographic system** for services at the Summer Olympic Games, 1979. Designed by Valeri Akopov, Mikhail Anikst, Vassily Diakonov, Andrey Kriukov, Igor Tikhomirov, Boris Trofimov and Alexander Shumilin, among others. For the 1980 Summer Olympic Games, designers from the Promgrafika (Industrial Graphics) department of the Moscow Artists Union developed a three-tiered pictographic system to help visitors find their way around the city and locate useful services. The system was highly regarded for its ingenious visual language and gained particular recognition from the international design community, including Ulm School of Design co-founder Otl Aicher. In 1982, it was awarded a Gold Medal at the International Biennale of Graphic Design in Brno, Czechoslovakia.

11

11 **Leningrad-80** biorhythm calculator with Olympic logotype, 1980.

12

12 **Wall clock** with pictograms of Olympic Sports, 1980. Manufactured by Yantar (Amber) Oryol Clock Factory. Nikolai Belkov designed twenty pictograms of Olympic sports for his senior project at Mukhina Arts School. He reconfigured the famous Otl Aicher pictograms from the 1972 Munich Olympics, softening them with smoother and more dynamic line intersections at 30 and 60 degrees, instead of Aicher's 45 and 90 degrees. The figures interact with the background and fit organically into a square or circular cell, making a unified silhouette that could be easily inverted when necessary.

13

13 **Technika Molodezhi** (Technology Youth) magazine, No. 7, 1962. Illustrations by D Pobedinsky, D Shumilin, and V Karabut, among others.

Игры
XXII Олимпиады
МОСКВА
1980
Games of the
XXII Olympiad
MOSCOW
1980
ДО НОВЫХ ВСТР

14

ч, ОЛИМПИАДА!

The main force in man – is the power of the spirit.

Ведь главная сила в человеке – это сила духа.

15

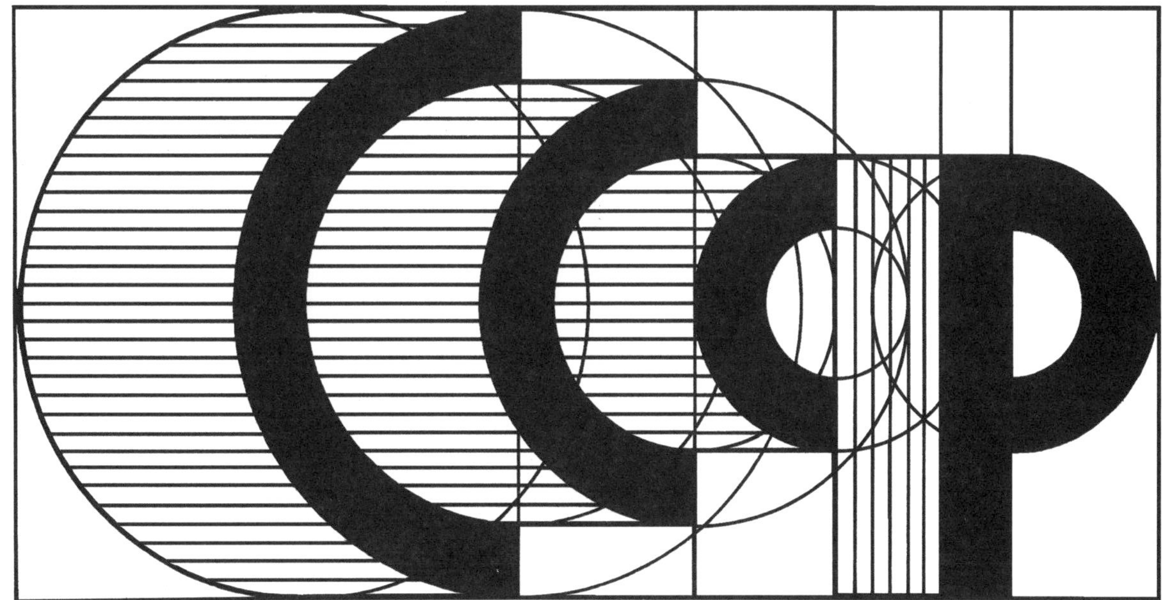

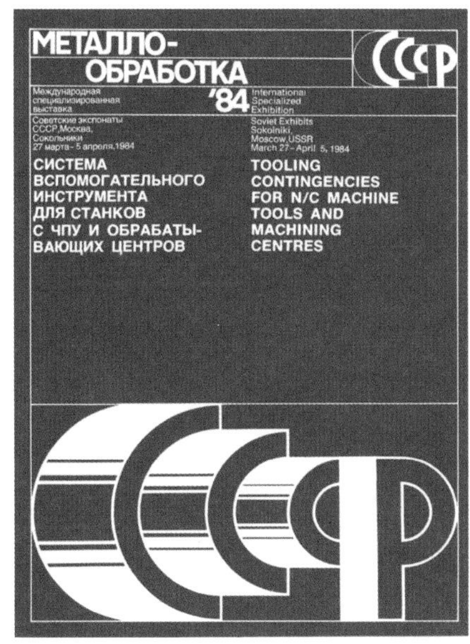

16

14 **Farewell, Olympic Games!** Olympic Games promotional poster, 1980. Designed by Miron Lukyanov.

15 – 16 **USSR Metalloobrabotka** (Metalworks) logo and promotional posters for the International Specialized Exhibition in Sokolniki, Moscow, 1984. Designed by Valeri Akopov, Evgeny Dobrovinski and Vasili Diakonov.

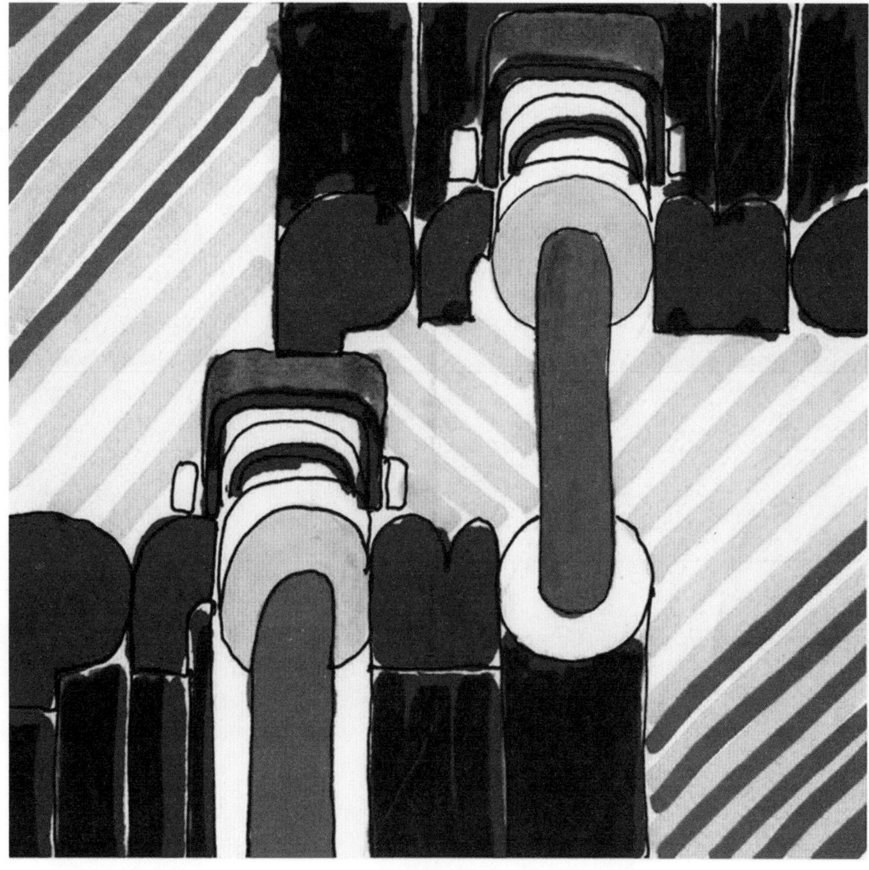

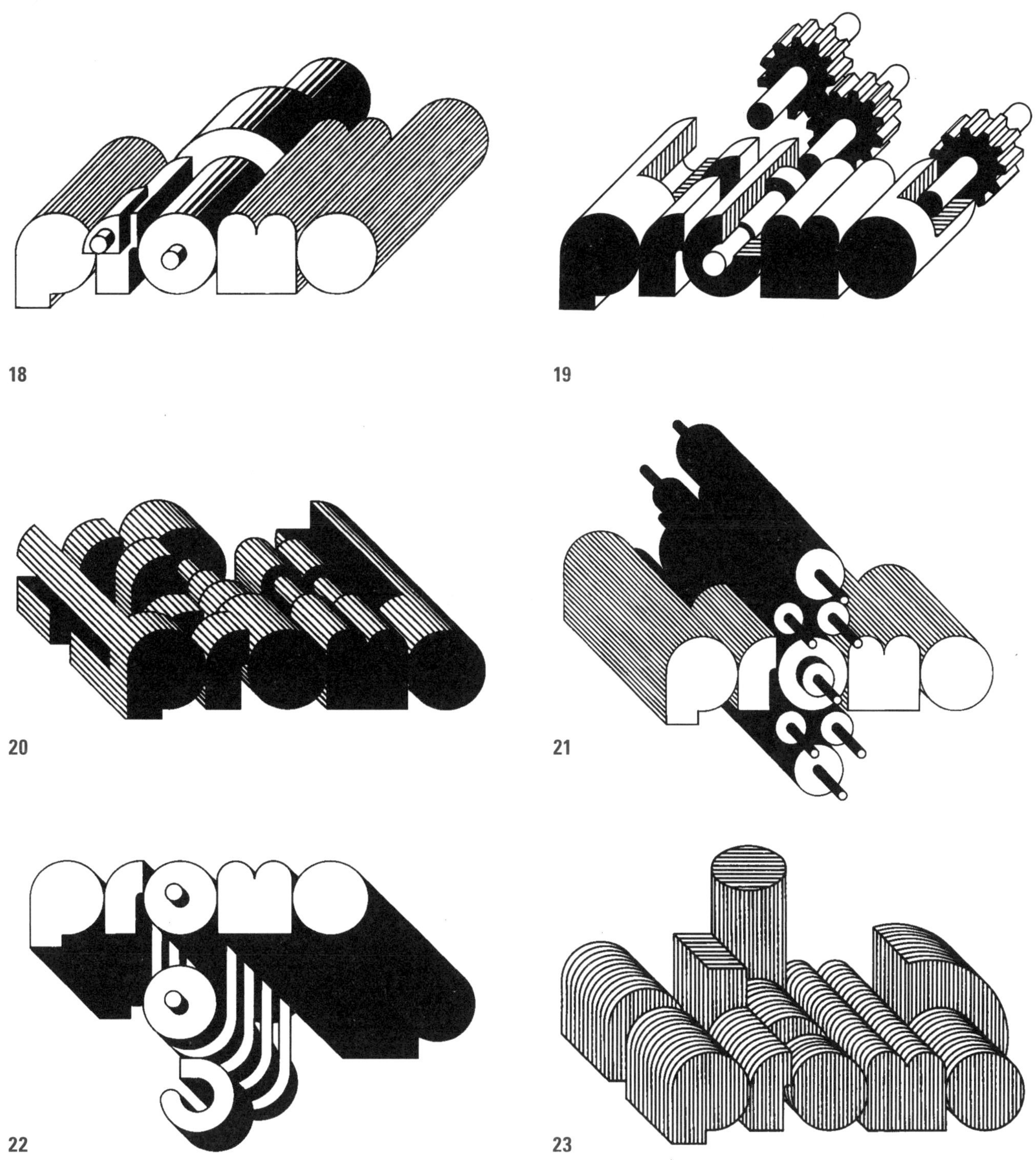

18 19 20 21 22 23

17 – 23 **Promo logotype series**, 1982. Designed by Valeri Akopov, Mikhail Anikst, Vasili Diakonov, Boris Trofimov and Aleksandr Shumilin, among others. In 1982, designers of the Promgrafika branch of VNIITE developed a logo and a series of advertising posters for the Prommasheksport Export Trade Association. From one base logotype they created fourteen variations signifying the association's different activities. These posters were awarded the Grand Prix at the International Biennale in Brno in 1986. The same principle of creating logos with dynamic features was later applied to eight other Soviet export trade associations.

24

24 **Krugozor** (Outlook) multimedia magazine, 1964–92. Manufactured by the Melodiya Record Firm. *Krugozor* was the first multimedia magazine to be released in the USSR. It launched in 1964 following the Soviet Union's purchase of French production technology that enabled the manufacture of flexible gramophone records. Each magazine contained up to six flexible, double-sided, seven-inch records, ranging from educational materials to popular music, including songs by international artists. From the late 1960s to the mid-1980s, *Krugozor* had a monthly print run of 500,000 copies and shaped the tastes of Soviet youth.

Кругозор
3
1966

25

25 **Yuri Gagarin's voice record** from *Krugozor* magazine, 1960s. Manufactured by the Melodiya Record Firm.

26

26 **Krugozor** multimedia magazine, 1964–92.
Manufactured by the Melodiya Record Firm.

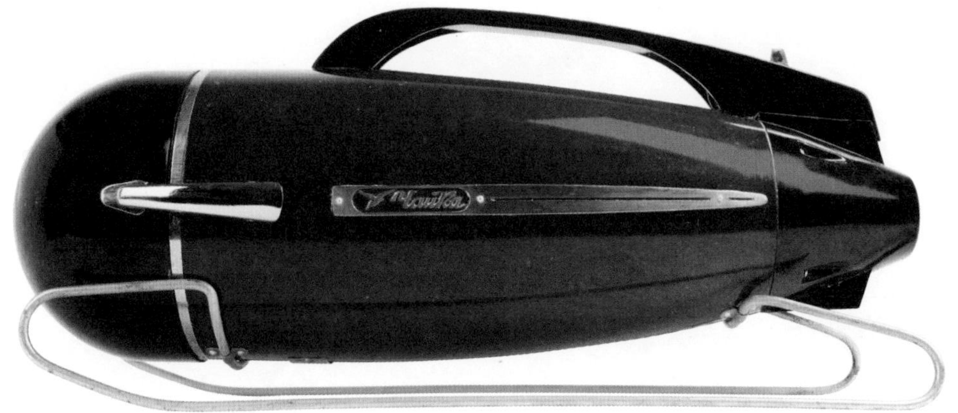

27

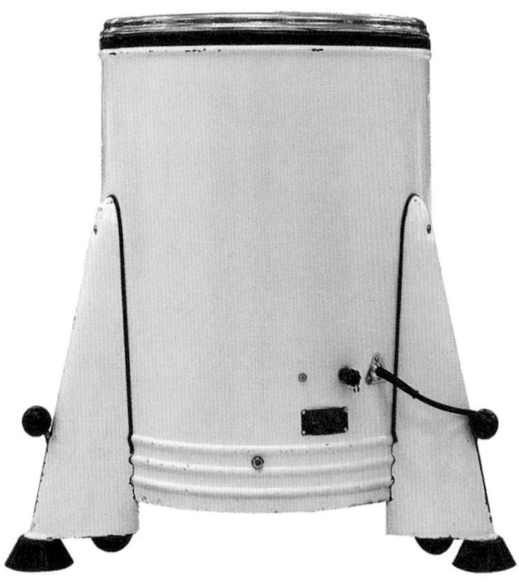

28

29

27 **Chaika** (Seagull) universal vacuum cleaner, 1950s. Manufactured by the Kommunar Machine Building Factory. It was not until 1952 that the USSR started to mass-produce vacuum cleaners, the earliest of which was was based on an Electrolux model from the 1930s. The Chaika vacuum cleaner had a more contemporary appearence that was inspired by a design from the Dutch brand Erres.

28 **Eaya 3** washing machine, 1951–5. Manufactured by the Electric Engineering Plant. The Eaya 3 was the first mass-produced Soviet home washing machine. It could wash and wring up to 2.5 kg (5.5 lbs) of dry laundry and is an interesting example of the space-age style in domestic product design.

29 **UP 1** vacuum cleaner, 1955. Manufactured by the Sergey Kirov Elektrosila Plant.

30

30 **Saturnas** vacuum cleaner, 1962–70s. Manufactured by the Welding Equipment Plant. A remarkable example of Soviet space-age design, the Saturnas was based on American company Hoover's Constellation vacuum cleaner, which debuted in 1955. However, unlike the Constellation, the Saturnas model was completely spherical and had a plastic ring around the body, making it appear more like a planet. In addition, the original air-powered base was replaced by wheels, giving the Saturnas greater mobility.

31

31 **Launching rocket nightlight**, 1960s.

32 **Through Worlds and Centuries** social awareness poster, 1965. Designed by Miron Lukyanov and Vasily Ostrovski.

через миры и века

33

33 **Belka and Strelka Space Adventurers** confectionery tin, 1960s. Manufactured by the Krasny Oktyabr Chocolate Factory. In 1951, the Soviet Union's space programme began to launch animals–mainly dogs and rabbits–into orbit around Earth, and many Soviet brands started to reflect these achievements. Laika the dog became one of the first animals to reach space during a 1957 launch, her extraordinary voyage sparking in a media sensation. Belka and Strelka, two other dogs whose space vehicle completed a full orbit around Earth in a 1960 launch, rose to even greater fame, having fortunately survived the journey. After the flight, Strelka even had puppies, one of which Soviet Secretary General Nikita Khrushchev gave as a gift to Jacqueline and Caroline Kennedy, the wife and daughter of US President John F Kennedy.

34

35

36

37

34 **Orbita** souvenir box, 1975.
35 **Sputnik** cigarette packaging, 1960s.
36 **Vostok 1** confectionery tin, 1960s.
37 **Kerchief packaging**, 1960–70s. Manufactured by the Sergei Kirov Textile and Thread Combine.

Long live indestructible friendship and cooperation.

Да здравствует нерушимая дружба и сотрудничество.

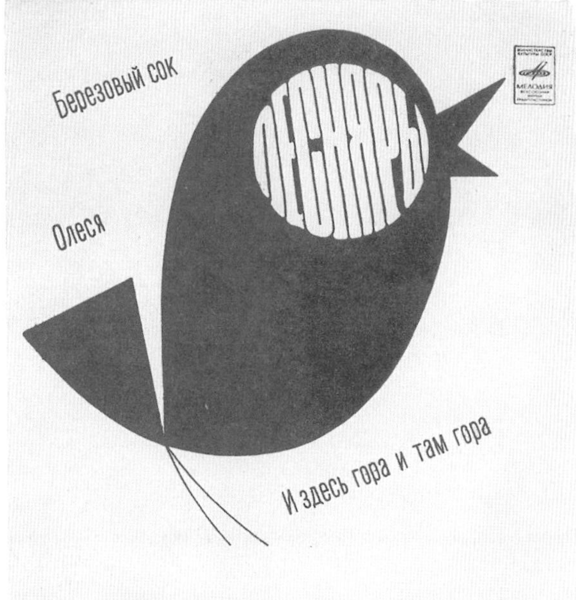

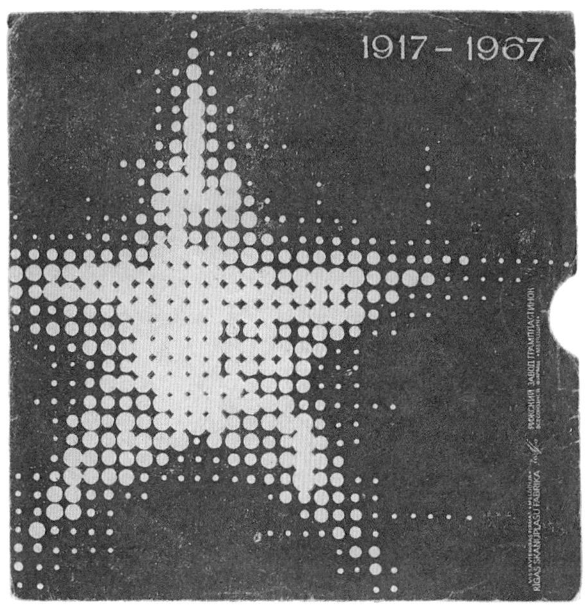

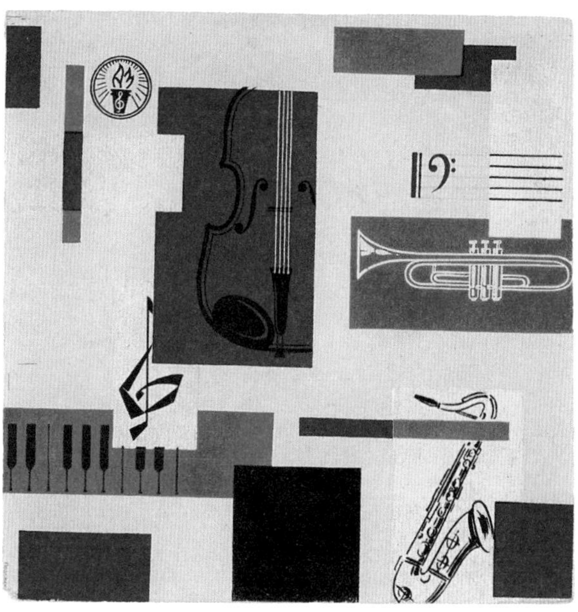

38

38 **7-inch record sleeves**, 1960–70s. Manufactured by the Melodiya Record Firm. In 1964, Melodiya integrated the majority of record manufacturing facilities and recording studios operating in the USSR, creating a monopoly on vinyl record production and distribution. The firm's records were exported to more than ninety countries and its covers were designed by a host of talented artists, members of the Union of Artists of the USSR and the Promgrafika design team. Unfortunately, the names of many designers working for the firm during that period are no longer known.

39

40

39 **Krunk** (Crane) double-necked electric guitar, 1975. Manufactured by the Yerevan Musical Instrument Plant. Since rock was considered ideologically alien in the USSR, the majority of musical instruments produced were folk and classical. It wasn't until the late 1960s that electric guitars became domestically available. The Krunk ('crane' in Armenian) was an original solution, combining a solo guitar and short-scale bass in one body. It is the only Soviet example of such an instrument. Other unusual instruments from this factory included an electric mandolin, launched in 1972.

40 **Turist 1** electric guitar, 1974. The Turist (Tourist) was most likely made at one of the defence industry's enterprises. It featured a built-in amplifying device with two speakers – perfect for taking on camping and day trips, which were popular Soviet leisure activities.

41

42

41 **Tonika** electric guitar, 1969. Manufactured by the Anatoly Lunacharsky Factory of Folk Musical Instruments. The Tonika was the first Soviet-designed electric guitar made in the USSR. The prototype was developed in 1964 with an upgraded version produced from 1969.

42 **Ural 650** electric guitar, 1977. Manufactured by the Ural Keyboard Instrument Factory. The Ural, based on a Japanese design, was the leading mass-produced electric guitar in the Soviet Union, with over 100,000 units manufactured. Soviet models were generally considered low-quality due to their poorly fitting components, heavy bodies and clumsy fingerboards. While imported electric guitars became available in the 1970s, they were too expensive for most people. Soviet models weren't cheap either, which is why homemade versions were a popular alternative.

43

43 **Slava** (Glory) table alarm clock, 1970–80s. Manufactured by the Slava Chelyabinsk Clock Factory. The Second Moscow Watch Factory (now known as Slava) began making timepieces in 1924. It has since become one of the best-known Russian watch brands, with its models exported to many countries worldwide. Some years, exports have comprised up to fifty per cent of the company's total production. Different product lines were introduced in the late 1950s, including women's, mechanical and quartz watches and alarm, pocket and wall clocks.

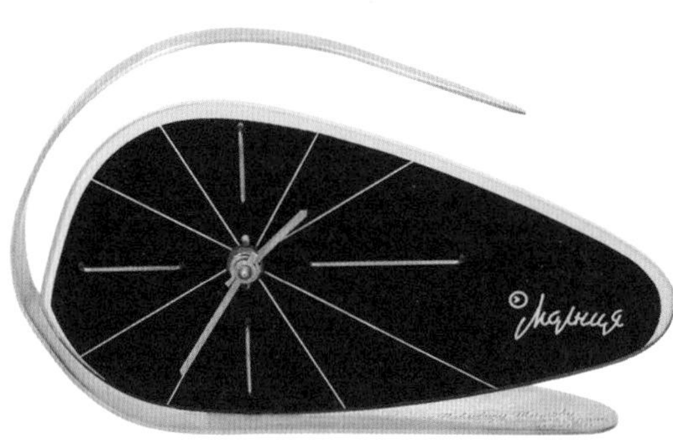

44

45

46

44 **Molniya** (Lightning) table clock, 1966. The Molniya Chelyabinsk Clock Factory operated from 1947 to 2007, initially producing industrial-scale timepieces for tanks, submarines and space vehicles for the Soviet Defence Ministry.

45 **Vostok 1** table clock, 1961. Manufactured by the Molniya Chelyabinsk Clock Factory.

46 **Table clock**, 1960s. Manufactured by the Yantar Oryol Clock Factory.

47

48

47 **Polot** (Flight) wristwatch with alarm, 1970s. Manufactured by the First Moscow Watch Factory.
48 **Polot** (Flight) wristwatch, 1970s. Manufactured by the First Moscow Watch Factory.
49 **Use Each Working Minute to Fulfil the Five-Year Plan** social awareness poster, 1970s. Designed by Konstantin Ivanov.

КАЖДУЮ
РАБОЧУЮ МИНУТУ
НА ВЫПОЛНЕНИЕ
ЗАДАНИЙ ПЯТИЛЕТКИ!

Fly higher, further and faster than anyone!

Летать выше, дальше и быстрее всех!

50

50 **Holiday with Zenith-E** export promotional poster, 1970–80s.

51

52

51 – 52 **Zenith-E** camera and Helios 44-2 lens packaging, 1960s. Manufactured by the Krasnogorsk Mechanical Factory and Belorussian Optical-Mechanical Association. The mass-exported Zenith-E was by far the most popular Soviet camera. More than 8 million of them were produced, setting something of a world record in producing cameras of this type.

53 **Zenith Avtomat** automatic camera, 1984–94. Designed by Vladimir Runge and Vladislav Shablevich, manufactured by the Krasnogorsk Mechanical Factory. This new-generation camera was equipped with most of the technical innovations of the 1980s: bayonet-mounted lens, electronically controlled shutter, aperture priority mode and a new high-aperture standard lens. It also incorporated an unusual assembly method that was

53

54

used for the first time in the USSR at the beginning of the 1970s while developing the Zenith-16. Instead of installing all the parts directly into the case, they were mounted on a metal frame and covered with pieces of high-strength plastic. This process improved assembly line efficiency and made mass production cheaper.

54 **Zenith-E** camera instuction manual, 1960s. Manufactured by the Krasnogorsk Mechanical Factory and Belorussian Optical-Mechanical Association.

55

56

57

58

55 **Zenith** camera, plastic mock-up, 1970–80s. Manufactured by the Krasnogorsk Mechanical Factory.

56 **Nartsiss** (Narcissus) miniature camera, 1961–5. Manufactured by the Krasnogorsk Mechanical Factory. The Nartsiss was allegedly the first 16 mm, single-lens reflex camera of its kind in the world. Orginally intended for use in medical and scientific fields, its high price meant that most were exported.

57 **Smena 8M** scale focus camera, 1970–90. Designed by Valentin Tsepov, manufactured by the Leningrad Optical Mechanical Association. The Smena (Switch) brand cameras were targeted to the mass consumer, so were cheap and easy to use. While lower quality than the Zenith, they were still popular among teen-agers and amateur photographers.

59

58 **Vilia** camera, 1974–85. Manufactured by the Belorussian Optical-Mechanical Association.

59 **Iskra** (Spark) folding camera, 1960–3. Manufactured by the Krasnogorsk Mechanical Factory.

60

61

62

63

60 **Svet DM-3** slide projector, 1972. Manufactured by the Omsk Electromechanical Plant.
61 **Avrora 215** movie camera, 1978–80s. Manufactured by the Leningrad Optical Mechanical Association.
62 **Sport 2** movie camera, 1961–5. Manufactured by the Leningrad Optical Mechanical Association.
63 **Lubitel** twin-lens reflex camera, 1950–6. Manufactured by the Leningrad Optical Mechanical Association.

64

65

64–65 **Kiev-30** miniature camera with leather case and packaging, 1975–87. Manufactured by the Arsenal Plant, State Enterprise of Special Instrumentation.

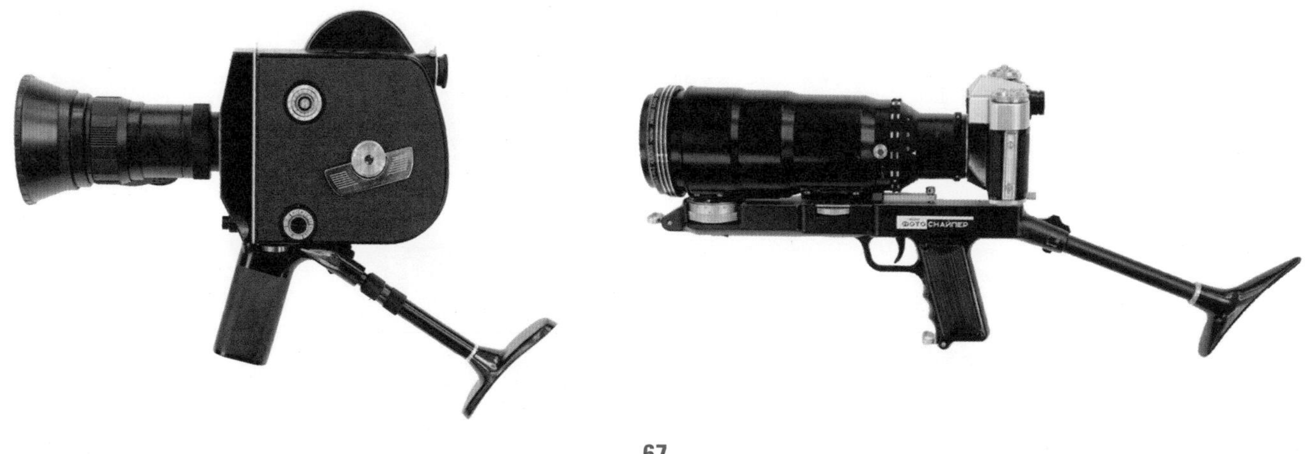

66

67

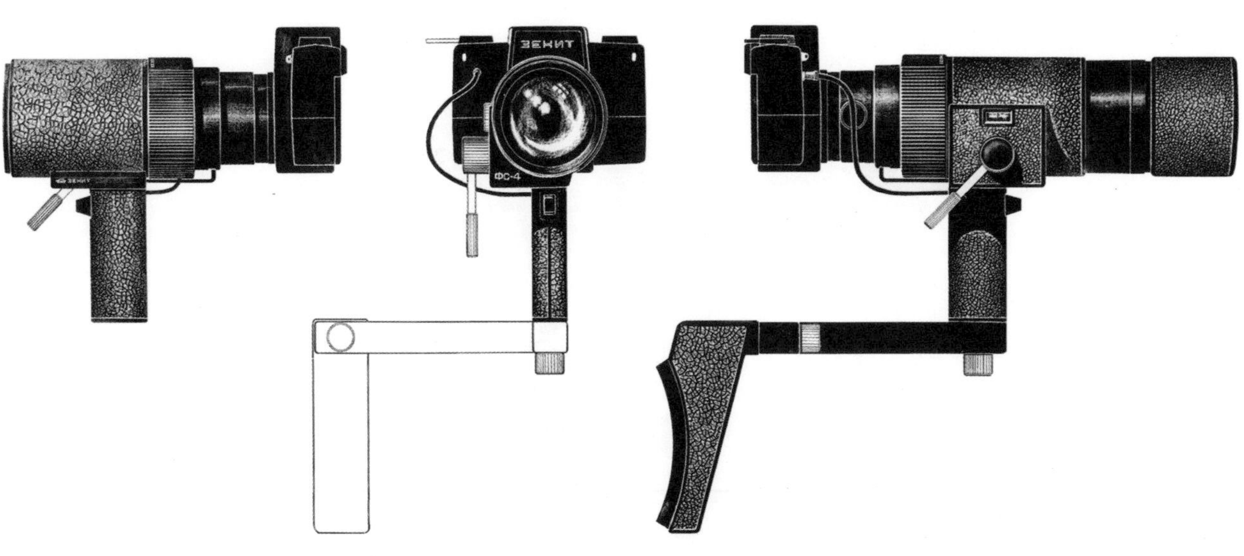

68

66 **Krasnogorsk-3** amateur movie camera, 1971–93. Designed by Evgeny Zherdev, manufactured by the Krasnogorsk Mechanical Factory. This was one of the most technologically advanced Soviet 16 mm movie cameras. Despite its amateur status, it was often used by professional operators at regional television studios.

67 **Photosniper FS-3** camera with detachable handle in the shape of a gun, 1965–82. Designed by S Malinski, manufactured by the Krasnogorsk Mechanical Factory. The Photosniper featured a telephoto lens, grip stock and shoulder stock. The first prototype models were used during World War II for gathering intelligence but the camera later became popular with photojournalists and nature photographers.

69

68 **Photosniper FS-3** sketches for redesign, 1970–80s. These sketches are the result of a collaboration between the Krasnogorsk Mechanical Factory and students of the Moscow State Stroganov University. The aim was to redesign the Photosniper to look like an optical tool rather than a weapon and also to improve the camera's ergonomics.

69 **Lomo Kompakt Avtomat** (LC-A) camera, 1983–2005. Designed by Valentin Tsepov, manufactured by the Leningrad Optical Mechanical Association. The Lomo was a 35 mm compact camera with automatic exposure. Its easy handling and durability made it hugely popular, giving rise to the international Lomography movement. Based on the Japanese Cosina CX-2, its design and function were reworked to add distinction.

70

70 **Technical Aesthetics** magazine covers, 1960–70s. *Technical Aesthetics* magazine was published by VNIITE from 1964 to 1992. It was the only monthly publication in the USSR dedicated entirely to design theory and practice. The term 'technical aesthetics' was used to denote design theory, and its use reflects the conceptual disposition toward this profession in the Soviet Union.

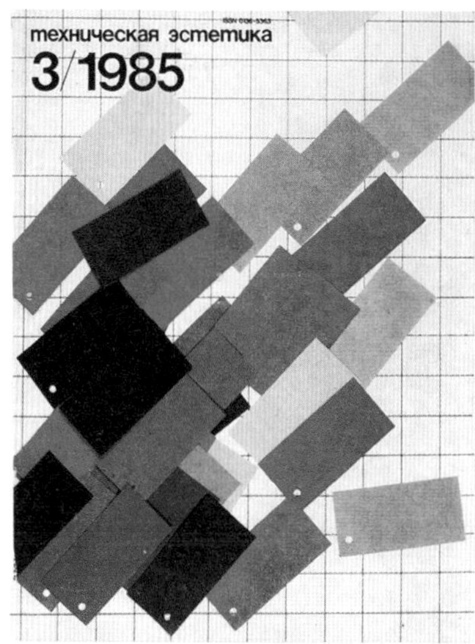

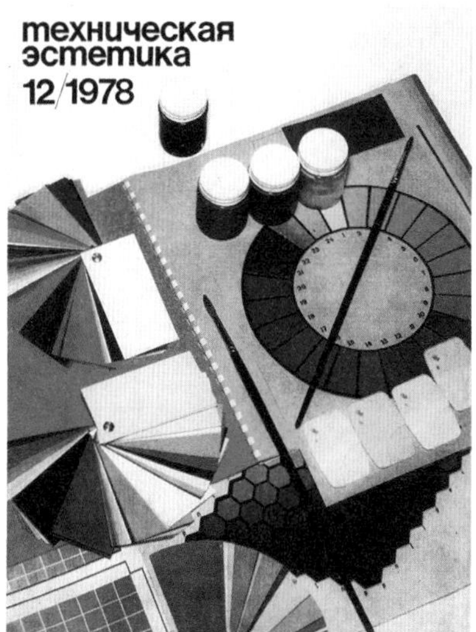

71

71 **Technical Aesthetics** magazine covers, 1970–80s.

72

72 **Technical Aesthetics** magazine cover, 1979.

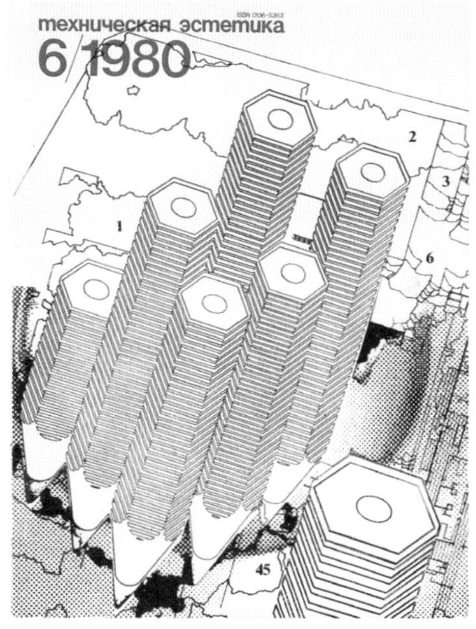

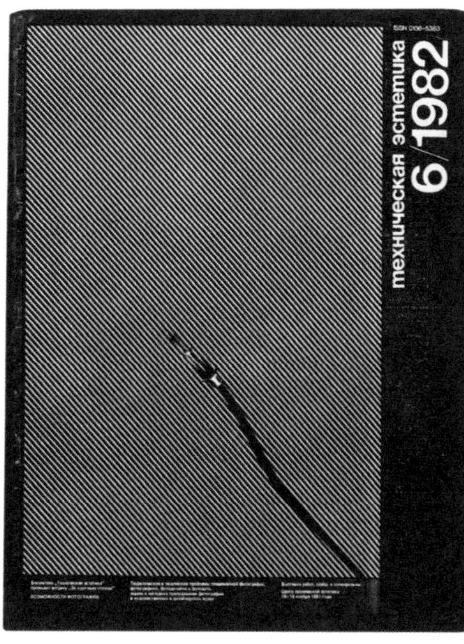

73

73 **Technical Aesthetics** magazine covers, 1970–80s.

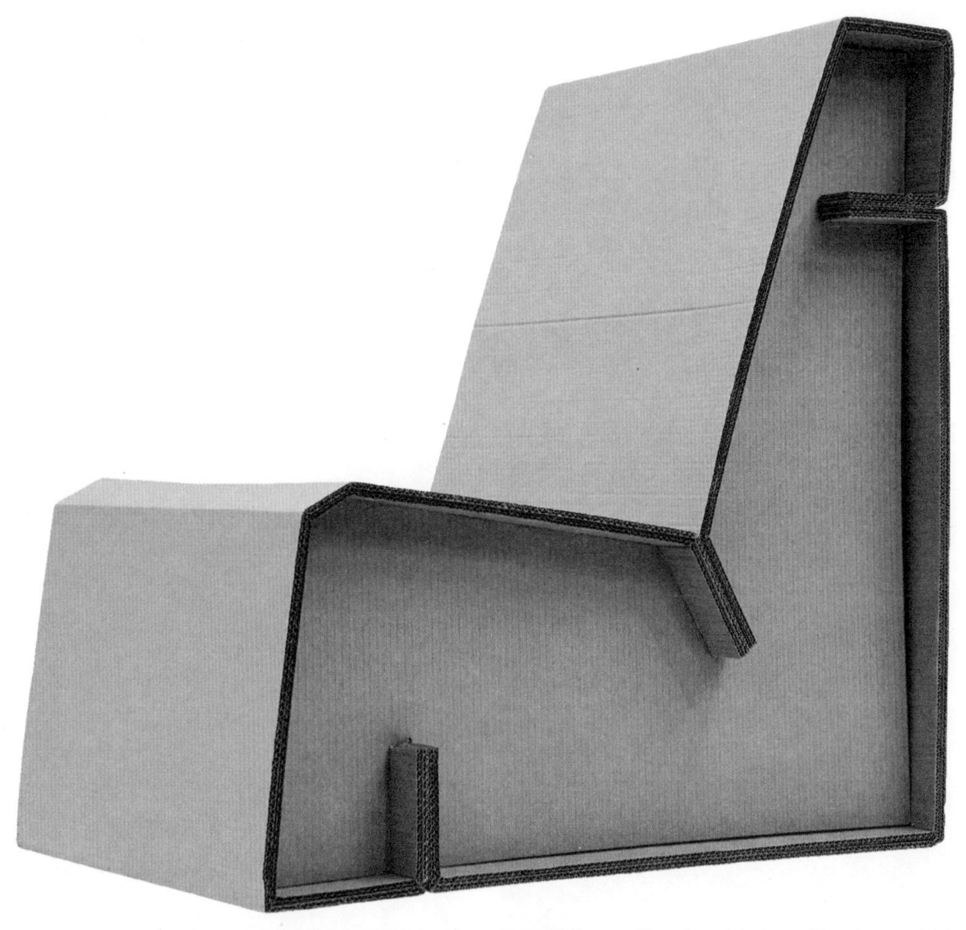

74

220 World

75

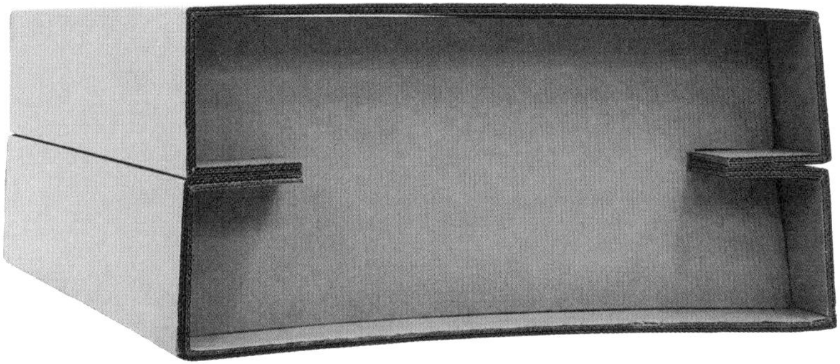

76

74 – 76 **Furniture set** stool, chair and table for the ICSID Congress, Moscow, 1975 (reproduction, 2012). In 1975, a team of designers from VNIITE, headed by Aleksander Ermolaev, developed a functional and original design for a set of cardboard furniture. It was exhibited in the public meeting areas of the International Council of Societies of Industrial Design (ICSID) Congress, a global conference for industrial designers. Each piece in the set, including the coffee table, chairs, stools, brochure stand, informational stand and rubbish bins, was assembled on site and could be easily moved around by congress attendees. This design solution allowed the organizers to create a democratic and creative atmosphere while utilizing minimal resources, demonstrating the sustainable nature of Soviet design.

77

SID'75ICSID'75I
MOSCOWMOS

ИНФОРМАЦ
БЮЛЛЕТЕНЬ
INFORMATIO
BULLETIN 1

ДИЗАЙН ДЛЯ ЧЕЛОВЕКА
И ОБЩЕСТВА
DESIGN FOR MAN
AND SOCIETY

78

Дизайн
и государственная
политика
Дизайн и наука
Дизайн и труд
Дизайн и отдых
Дизайн для детей
Дизайн
для инвалидов
и престарелых

Design
and State Policy
Design and Science
Design and Labour
Design and Leisure
Design for Children
Design
for the Handicapped
and the Ageing

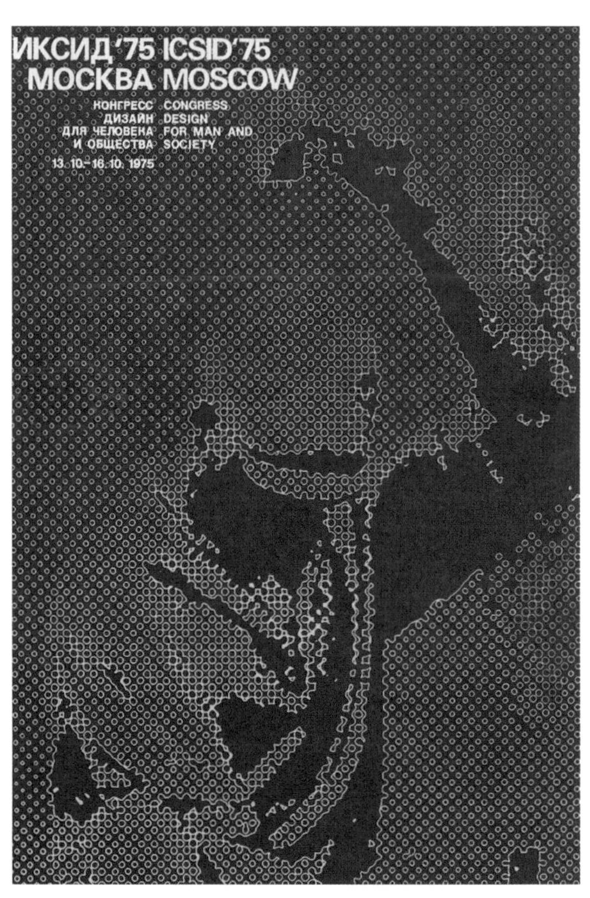

79

77 – 78 **Brochures and posters** for the ICSID Congress, Moscow, 1975. Designed by Igor Berezovski.

79 – 80 **Corporate ephemera** for the ICSID Congress, Moscow, 1975. Designed by Igor Berezovski, Yevgeni Bogoanov, Viktor Zenkov and Aleksander Ermolaev. VNIITE designers were ahead of their time, applying the principles of dynamic identity to the corporate branding for the '75 ICSID Congress in Moscow. Instead of developing a traditional logo, they created a flexible system using photographs of individuals differentiated by several graphic filters. These could then be placed freely within the space of corporate ephemera to create a feeling of movement. This graphic solution was inspired by the theme of the congress – Design for People and Society.

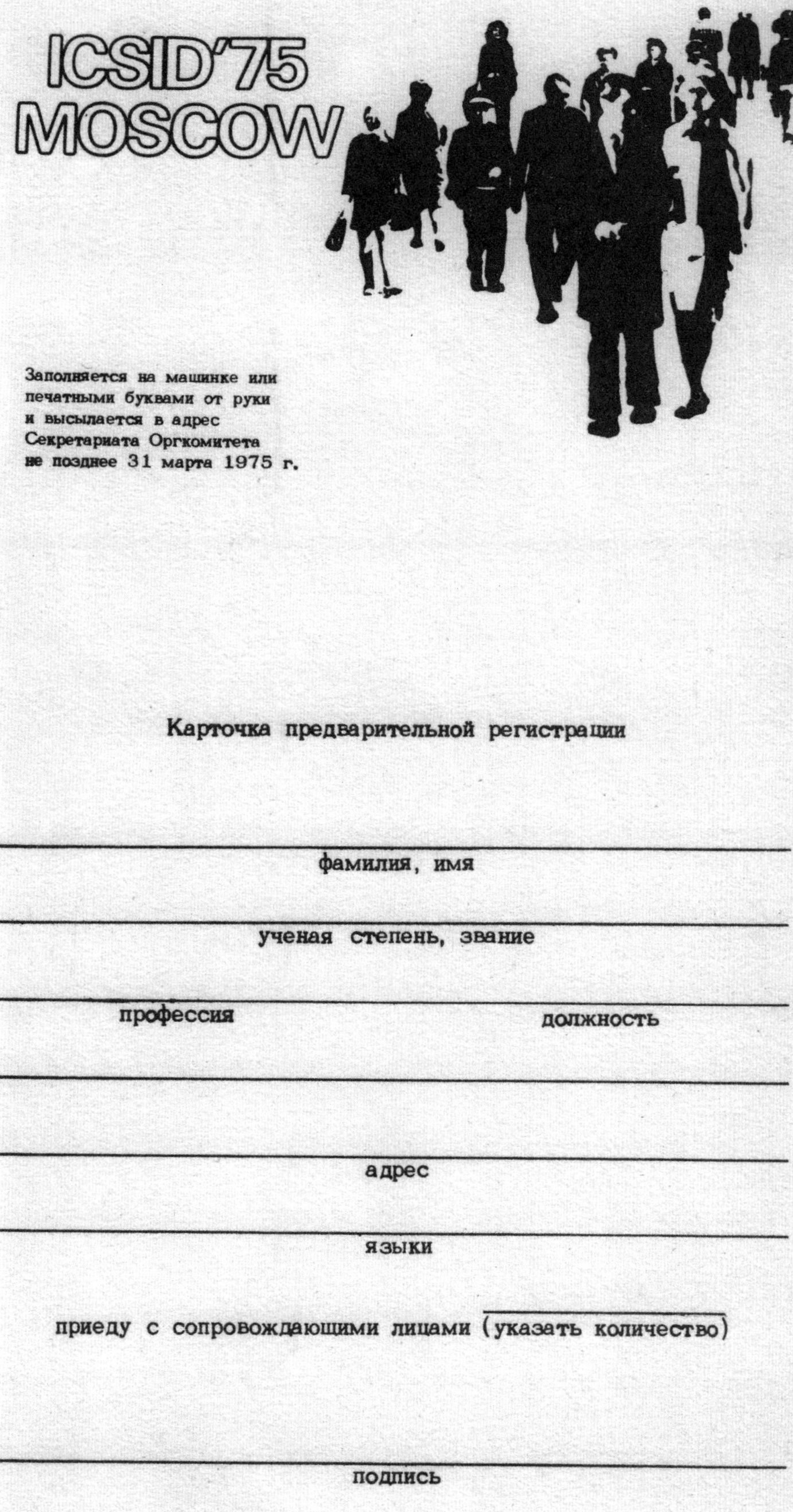

Заполняется на машинке или
печатными буквами от руки
и высылается в адрес
Секретариата Оргкомитета
не позднее 31 марта 1975 г.

Карточка предварительной регистрации

фамилия, имя

ученая степень, звание

профессия | должность

адрес

языки

приеду с сопровождающими лицами (указать количество)

подпись

дата

81

16 00
21-89

82

81 – 82 **VNIITE-PT** (Perspective Taxi) project, 1963–5. Designed by Yuri Dolmatovski, Alexander Ol'shanetski and A Chernyayev (VNIITE). The design of this personalized taxi was ahead of its time – it embodied the idea of a public transport vehicle with the characteristics of a private car. Only two models were ever produced, one of which was tested for one month, driving around Moscow and picking up customers. Following this test run, the model was recommended for pre-production but unfortunately, the project never came to fruition. Some of the innovative design solutions, such as a carriage-type body with a rear-engine layout and sliding doors, were later used in designs developed in the West. One example is the conceptual 1976 Alfa Romeo New York Taxi, presented by Ital Design studio for an exhibition at the Museum of Modern Art, New York.

83

84

83 – 84 **Zil-Sides VMA 30** fire truck, 1975. Designed by Vladimir Ariamov, Lev Kuz'michev, Alexander Ol'shanetski and T Shepeleva (VNIITE). At the beginning of the 1970s, VNIITE designers, along with the All-Union Research Institute for Fire Prevention, began work on an innovative new design for a fire engine. The truck had a carriage-type car body with a rear-engine layout, sliding doors, easily accessible low steps and an unconventional overall appearance. The centrally located water pump unit could be launched while the truck was in motion, allowing firefighters to take action from the moment they arrived on site.

85

85 **Vyatka VP-150** scooter, 1957–66. Designed by Igor Zaitsev, manufactured by the Molot (Hammer) Vyatka-Polyansky Engineering Plant. The Vyatka VP-150 was the first Soviet scooter. Its design was based entirely on the iconic Vespa 150 GS Italian scooter, designed in 1955. In the same year, production also began of the Tula T-200 scooter, which was based on the East German Goggo-roller TA200 scooter by Hans Glas GmbH. Other later models were the Turist (Tourist) and Tulitsa scooters. Interestingly, both plants responsible for manufacturing scooters in the USSR were employed by the defence industry.

86

86 **Belka A50** (Squirrel) compact car project, 1955–6. Prototype designed by Yuri Dolmatovsky, Vladimir Aryamov, Zeyvang K, K Korzinkin and A Oksentevich. This innovative passenger car resulted from a collaboration between designers of the Scientific Research Automobile and Engine Institute (NAMI) and the Irbit Motorcycle Plant (IMZ). Due to the front panel door and a carriage-type car body, this compact model fit four passengers. It also utilized many technological advancements of its time and had an alternative configuration featuring an open-top car body. Unfortunately, only five cars were ever produced. One reason for this was that the Soviet government instead chose to follow a 'proven design solution' set by the Italian FIAT-600 city car, which became the basis for the famous series of ZAZ-965 cars produced from 1958.

87

87 **Latvija RAF-977 minibus** advertising brochures 1959–76. Designed by Svetlana Mirzoyan, manufactured by the Riga Bus Factory. The production of minibuses in the USSR began in 1957. Drawing inspiration from analogous Volkswagen models, Svetlana Mirzoyan quickly developed a design for the RAF-977. It survived for several decades with only slight alterations and variations. Passenger, freight and ambulance versions of the vehicle were produced for domestic and foreign markets. The RAF-977 received awards at prestigious motor shows in London (1960), Brussels (1961) and Paris (1962).

88

88 **Aeroflot** promotional brochures, 1960s.

Design in the USSR

'Regarding Soviet design, there are, of course, peculiarities, historical ones. There was a period when the word "design" was a bad word – not just the word, but the activity itself.' – Igor Zaitsev

'The main feature of the Soviet school of design was its humanistic approach.' – Vladimir Runge

'When there was a shortage of consumer goods, the formula 'that will do' seemed natural. Almost every Soviet object and environment corresponded to this formula.' – Alexander Ermolayev

'While preparing their collections, the Riga Fashion House went to the Library of Foreign Literature to borrow issues of *Vogue* or *Harper's Bazaar* and secretly copied designs on tracing paper, holding the magazines on their knees.' – Alexandre Vassiliev

'The Soviet school of design consists of two eternally split and tragically broken lives; the first one is the Russian avant-garde, the second is VNIITE. What unites them is that their driving force and artistic method were an impossible dream.' – Dmitry Azrikan

'In those years, we wanted to rearrange what was left of the old world and make the things we designed understandable, lively and, most importantly, ours.' – Mark Konik

'There was a story that a 16 mm Soviet video camera fell off the Eiffel Tower, and when it was picked up from the lawn, it was still working. One could not think of a better advertisement for Soviet goods.' – Vladimir Runge

'Soviet designers worked in a state institution with a censorship system – many designs were rejected as not Soviet enough, not ideologically stable enough or not moral enough.' – Alexandre Vassiliev

'Remarkably, at that time, design in the USSR was the second hole in the Iron Curtain. The first one was jazz. Youth cafés were the venue for jazz, and VNIITE was the venue for design.' – Dmitry Azrikan

'We moved toward graphic design almost instinctively, like blind people in the dark. It seemed to us that it had existed in the West for a long time, but when we actually got to meet the idols of our youth, our European and American colleagues, it turned out that we entered this profession almost at the same time.' – Valeri Akopov

Valeri Akopov (b. 1938) is a graphic designer. He was chairman of the Promgrafika (industrial graphics) department of the Moscow Union of Artists from 1958–93 and throughout his career has participated in many exhibitions, both in Russia and worldwide. He founded is own studio, Akopov Design, in 1992.

Manuil Andreev (1884–1959) was a graphic designer and illustrator who worked at the Red October Factory.

Mikhail Anikst (b. 1938) is a graphic designer, illustrator and artist, best known for his work as chief artist at the Sovietsky Khudozhnik Publishing House, where he produced many memorable advertising posters. At the end of the 1970s he joined the Promgrafika studio to help in the development of pictograms for the 1980 Summer Olympics.

Dmitry Azrikan (b. 1934) obtained a PhD in fine art before pursuing a career as a designer and teacher. He studied and worked at VNIITE throughout the 1960s–80s and was head of the institute's design programme from 1973–88. Azrikan founded the USSR's first independent industrial design studio in 1980, which he ran for more than a decade before emigrating to the US to become an associate professor at Western Michigan University. He currently works independently as an exhibition designer.

Victor Chizhikov (b. 1935) is a children's book illustrator, best known for designing the 1980 Summer Olympic Games mascot, Misha the Bear.

Yuri Dolmatovsky (1913–99) was an industrial designer who held a PhD in engineering. He was head of automobiles at the Soviet Academy of Science and was also on the board of studies at the Faculty of Modern Engineering at the People's University of Moscow.

Aleksander Ermolaev (b. 1941) is a designer, architect and teacher. He was a member of VNIITE for over twenty years and founded his own studio TAF in 1980. He has been a professor in the Design of an Architectural Environment department at the Moscow Architectural Institute (MARCHI) since 1988.

Alexander Grashin (b. 1936) is a designer, design theorist and educator. He was a professor at the Russian Academy of Natural Sciences and the European Academy of Natural Sciences.

Adolf Irbitis (1910–83) was an industrial designer who developed many of the Soviet Union's most recognized electronic products. He worked as a designer at the VEF Radio Factory from 1941, rising to chief industrial designer in 1956.

Alexei Kolotushkin (b. 1956) is an industrial designer who worked in the department of design techniques at VNIITE from 1984–9.

Mark Konik (1938–2013) was a designer, artist and teacher. Between 1964–91 he worked at the Senezh Studio – an experimental education organization – first as a scientific adviser and then as head of environmental design.

Andrey Krukov (1923–97) was a designer who worked as art director at the Melodiya Record Firm and from 1960–80 was head of the Promgrafika department of the Moscow Union of Artists – an organization responsible for designing logos and corporate identities of all factories and industrial businesses in the USSR.

Alexander Lavrentyev (b. 1954) is a designer, historian and curator, specializing in design and photography theory. He holds a PhD in fine art and is currently vice-president of research at the Stroganov Moscow State Academy of Arts and Industry, where he is also a professor of communication design.

Alla Levashova (1918–74) was a fashion designer and the first person in the USSR to set up a ready-to-wear collection at the All-Union Fashion House in Moscow. She is also credited with the beginnings of mass-produced Soviet clothing.

Miron Lukyanov (1936–2007) was a graphic designer, artist and member of the Moscow Union of Artists. He was also a prolific movie-poster designer and joined the State Surikov Academy as a professor in 1994.

Maria Maistrovskaya (b. 1947) worked as a furniture designer at the All-Union Institute for Furniture Design and Technology from 1974–7. She is currently a professor at Stroganov Moscow State University of Arts and Industry and chief researcher at the Research Institute of Art History and Theory at the Russian Academy of Arts.

Tatiana Mavrina (1900–96) was an artist and children's book illustrator who drew inspiration from Russian folk art and culture.

Svetlana Mirzoyan (b. 1936) is a designer, design theorist and educator. She holds a PhD in fine art and is a professor at the Stieglitz Saint Petersburg State Academy of Arts and Industry.

Vladimir Runge (b. 1937) is a designer and design historian. In 1965 he established the design department at the Krasnogorsk Mechanical Factory, which he ran until 1987. He was also a professor at the Russian Academy of Natural Sciences.

Alexandra Sankova (b. 1979) is a design historian, curator and lecturer and has worked as the director of the Moscow Design Museum since 2012. Her curatorial projects include: *Soviet Design, 1950–1980*, Moscow Design Museum, 2012 (travelling); *Russia. Bread. Salt.*, Milan Expo, 2015; *Discovering Utopia: Lost Archives of Soviet Design*, London Design Biennale, 2016; and *Paper Revolution*, ADAM, Brussels, 2017, among many others.

Vera Sklyarova (1908–76) was a textile designer at the Moscow Textile Factory and chief editor of the women's fashion magazine published by the All-Union Fashion House.

Yuri Sluchevskiy (1928–2017) was an industrial and furniture designer and writer, authoring several books on design throughout his career. From 1957, he was a professor at Stroganov Moscow State University of Arts and Industry and in 1975 joined as head of the All-Union Institute of Furniture Design and Technology.

Alyona Sokolnikova (b. 1984) is a curator and has worked as head of research projects at the Moscow Design Museum since 2012. She is also an associate professor at Sholokhov Moscow State University of Humanities. Her curatorial projects include: *British Design: From William Morris to the Digital Revolution*, Pushkin Museum, Moscow, 2014; and *Soviet Design, 1950–1980*, Moscow Design Museum, 2012 (travelling).

Yuri Soloviev (1920–2013) was a designer. He founded and was the director of VNIITE and the USSR Association of Designers. He also held the position of president of the International Council of Societies of Industrial Design.

Kirill Sukhanov (b. 1954) is a designer who worked at the Souzprodoformlenie – an organization specializing in packaging design.

Boris Trofimov (b. 1940) is a graphic designer who co-founded the Higher Academic School of Graphic Design, where he was also a professor. Since 2013 he has worked as head of graphic design at the Institute of Business and Design.

Aleksandre Vassiliev (b. 1958) is a fashion historian, collector and television presenter. Since 2008 he has been chairman of the board of trustees for the National Museum of Fashion, Riga.

Igor Zaitsev (b. 1939) was chief designer at the Leninist Communist Youth Union Automobile Plant from 1974–87. He joined the Moscow Union of Designers as vice-president in 1999 and was also docent at the Moscow State University of Mechanical Engineering.

Vyacheslav Zaitsev (b. 1938) is a fashion designer, painter, graphic artist and theatrical costume designer. He was the artistic director of experimental technical garment factory, Mosoblsovnarkhoza, and chief designer at the All-Union Fashion House. In 1982 he established is own Moscow-based fashion house, Slava Zaitsev, and is the first Soviet couturier to be permitted by the Soviet Government to label his own clothing.

A
Abava RP 8330 portable transistor radio 120, *120*
Aeroflot promotional brochure 233, *233*
Afera V Kazino movie poster 131, *132*
Akkord transistor electrophone 111, *111*
Alyonka chocolate wrappers 15, *15*
Anton, Masha and Grib Nevalyashka roly-poly dolls 82, *82*
Antract sweet wrapper 12, *12*
AT-100s soda water vending machine 165, *165*
Atmosfera portable transistor radio 114, *114*, 116
Avos'ka string shopping bag 66, *66*
Avrora 215 movie camera 212, *212*
Avrora wired radio 115, *115*

B
baby carriage 87, *87*
bags 32, 60, 66, 99–101
Balalaika gift box 88, *88*
Ballet face powder box 53, *53*
beach series ceramic figurine 65, *65*
beer cans 40, *40*
Belaya Noch cigarette tin 44, *44*
Belka A50 compact car 231, *231*
Belka and Strelka Space Adventurers confectionery tin 196, *196*
Belochka sweet wrapper 12, *12*
Beloe Solntse Pustyni movie poster 145, *145*
Beregis Avtomobilya movie poster 140, *140*, *148–9*, 150
Bez Strakha I Upreka movie poster 131, *131*
biorhythm calculators 179, *179*
books 93, *93*
breakfast crackers 28, *28*
brochures, promotional 22–3, 161–4, 222–4, 232–3
Buratino plastic toy 89, *89*

C
cameras 207–15
cars: Belka A50 231, *231*
GAZ-69 toy car 81, *81*
Moskvich C-1 147, *147*
Moskvich 408 147, *147*
remote control car 79, *79*
toy pedal cars 78, *78*
VNIITE-PT project *226–7*, 228, *228*
Volga GAZ-M21 *150*, 151, *151*
caviar tin 27, *27*
ceramics 64–5
Chai Gruzinsky Extra 27, *27*
Chai Krasnodarsky Extra 27, *27*
Chaika 4 television set 122, *122*
Chaika universal vacuum cleaner 192, *192*
Cheburashka toys 86, *86*
Chernaya Chaika movie poster 134, *134*
Chernie Ochki movie poster 135, *135*
chess 98–9
Chipolino plastic toy 91, *91*
Chistye Prudy movie poster 134, *134*
chocolate wrappers 15, 17–21
Christmas tree gift box 88, *88*
Chvanchkara Georgian wine label 34, *34*
cigarette packaging 44–5, 197
Cinandali Georgian wine label 36, *36*
clocks 99, 180, 202–3
clothing, athletic uniform for the torch replay 174, *174*
cocoa packaging 38, *38*
coffee grinders 30, *30*, 75, *75*
coffee tins, instant 31, *31*
Cognac boxes 38, *38*
collapsible cup for liquids 165, *165*
combine harvester prototype 155, *155*
combs 60, *60*
confectionery tins 33, *33*
construction kits 87, 109
containers, enamel 75, *75*
corporate ephemera 224, *224–5*
Crown cap 164–5, *164*

D
Dagvino souvenir Cognac boxes 38, *38*
dairy bottles 25, *25*
Designers Society of the USSR 161, *162–3*
desk fans 71, *71*
Detski children's tooth powder 27, *27*
Devuskha S Knigoi ceramic figurine 65, *65*
dog soft toy 83, *83*
dolls 82, 87
Dozhdlivoe Voskresen'e movie poster *128*, 129
draughts set, portable magnetic 99, *99*
Drug Moi, Kol'ka! movie poster 131, *133*
Dymok perfume bottle 54, *54*

E
Eaya 3 washing machine 192, *192*
egg carriers 67, *67*
electric iron 68, *68*
Electronika 324/1 portable cassette player and recorder 121, *121*
Electronika 591 portable colour reel-to-reel video tape recorder 124, *125*
Electronika T802 modular radio construction kit 109, *109*
Electronika TS-401 M portable television set 124, *124*
Electronika VL100 portable television set 123, *123*
electrophones 110–11
Elfa 6-1M portable valve reel-to-reel tape recorder 110, *111*
enamel containers 75, *75*
Era-2M miniature radio 117, *117*
Ereti Georgian wine label 34, *34*

F
fabric swatches 46–8
face powder 53, 55
fairy tale books 93, *93*
figurines: ceramic 65, *65*
mascot 177, *177*
fire truck, Zil-Sides VMA 30 229, *229*
flip calendar 139, *139*
forklift truck model prototype 155, *155*
fox in a folk costume 91, *91*
fox soft toy 83, *83*
furniture set *220*, 221

G
Gagarin, Yuri, voice recording 190, *190*
games 98–9
GAZ-12 ZIM remote control car 79, *79*
GAZ-69 toy car 81, *81*
gift boxes 88, *88*
gift sets 43, *43*
girl in a dress squeaky rubber doll 89, *89*
Golysh Pups baby doll 87, *87*
guitars 200–1
guns, Kalashnikov toy 141, *141*

H
handbags 60, *60*
hats 96, *96*
headphones 124, *124*
heavy goods vehicle prototype 155, *155*
Helios 44-2 lens packaging 208, *208*
hockey stick 97, *97*
hydro-copying machines 156–8

I
ICSID Congress brochures and posters (1975) *222*, *223*, 224
instruction manuals, camera *209*
integrated communicative systems 159, *159*
irons 68, *68*
Iskra folding camera 211, *211*
jewellery box, lipstick 60, *60*

K
Kalashnikov toy gun 141, *141*
Kamaz wooden toy truck 90, *90*
Kamenniy Tsvetok perfume bottle 53, *53*
Kapitanskiy pipe tobacco 44, *44*
Kara-Kum chocolate wrapper 17, *17*
Kem Bit? construction kit 87, *87*
kerchief packaging 197, *197*
Khoziaistvennie matches 39, *39*
Kiev-30 miniature camera 213, *213*
Kogo My Bolshe Lyubim movie poster 135, *135*
Kometa MG-201 valve reel-to-reel tape recorder 110, *110*
Kosmos portable radio 116, *117*
Krasnaya Moskva face powder box 53, *53*
Krasnaya Moskva perfume 51, *51*
Krasnogorsk-3 amateur movie camera 214, *214*
Kreker K Zavtraku breakfast crackers 28, *28*
Kremlovskaya Vertushka STA-2 telephone 129, *129*
Krokodil Gena toys 86, *86*
Krugozor multimedia magazine 188–91
Krunk double-necked electric guitar 200, *200*

L
Lakomka sweet wrapper 17, *17*
lamps, reserve lamp for the Olympic flame 175, *175*
Latvija RAF-977 minibus 232, *232*
launching rocket nightlight 194, *194*
Leningrad chocolate wrapper 20, 21
Leningrad-80 biorhythm calculator 179, *179*
Leningrad T-2 television and radio set 122, *122*
lighting 72–3, 194
Limonaya bitter liqueur label 42, *42*
lipstick jewellery box 60, *60*
Lomo Kompakt Avtomat camera 215, *215*
Lubitel twin-lens reflex camera 212, *212*

M
magazines 56–9, 125–7, 181, 188–91, 216–19
magnetic tape packaging 176, *177*
Mari El skis 97, *97*
Marshrut 99 movie poster 142–3, 144
mascot figurines 177, *177*
matchboxes 39, *39*
Meteor sweet wrapper 17, *17*
Micro miniature radio 117, *117*
milk cartons 24, *24*
minibus, Latvija RAF-977 232, *232*
Minpisheprom 42, *42*
Mir sweet wrapper 16, *16*
Mishka Na Severe 19, *19*
Modeli Odezhdi magazine 59, *59*
modeling clay kit for children 95, *95*
Modi Tkani magazine 59, *59*
Mokko sweet wrapper 17, *17*
Molniya table clock 203, *203*
Molodo-Zeleno movie poster 135, *135*
mosaic kits 94, *94*
Moskva cigar packaging 45, *45*
Moskvich 408 car 147, *147*
Moskvich C-1 car model 147, *147*
Moskvich toy pedal car 78, *78*
Moskvich wired radio 115, *115*
movie cameras 212, 214
movie posters 128–38, 140, 142–5, 150, 166–7
Mukuzani Georgian wine label 36, *36*

N
Na Lednike Fedchenko movie poster 166, *166*
Nartsiss miniature camera 210, *210*
Natasha perfume packaging 52, *52*
nightlight, launching rocket 194, *194*
Novie Tovari magazine 125, *126*, *127*

O
Odezhda I Bit magazine 58, *58*
Olympic Games 172–85
Misha the Bear mascot 176–7
Olympic Games promotional poster *172–3*, 174
Olympic sports mosaic kit 94, *94*
pictographic system for Summer Olympic Games 178, *178*
Olympic Torch Relay: athletic sneakers for the torch relay 175, *175*
Olympic torch 175, *175*
reserve lamp for the Olympic flame 175, *175*
Orbita souvenir box 197, *197*

P
packaging *see* sweet wrappers; tins, *et*pasta packaging 29, *29*
perfume bottles and packaging 51–4
Petushok Zolotoy Grebeshok chocolate wrapper 18, *18*
Photosniper FS-3 camera 214, *214*, 215
pictographic system for Summer Olympic Games 178, *178*
plastic bag 66, *66*
Polet cigarette packaging 45, *45*
Polot wristwatch 204, *204*
Posle Svadbi movie poster 144, *144*
postcards 15, *15*
posters: movie posters 128–38, 140, 142–5, 150, 166–7
Olympic Games *172–3*, 174, *182–3*, 185
promo logotype series *186*, 187
promotional 207, *222*, *223*, 224
social awareness posters 104–7, 146–7, 164–9, 194, *195*, 204, *205*
USSR Metalloobrabotka logo and posters 185, *185*
Waiting for Instructions from the Centre *138*, 139
Prazdnichni Nabor festive gift set 43, *43*
Prima cigarette packaging 45, *45*
promo logotype series *186*, 187
Pshenichnaya vodka labels 42, *42*
Pudra-Listochki face powder 55, *55*

R
radio construction kits 109, *109*
radiola 110–12
radios 113–20, 122, 124
raisin tins 75, *75*
record sleeves 199, *199*
refrigerator manuals 77, *77*
remote control car 79, *79*
rice tins 75, *75*
Riga 60 washing machine 69, *69*
Riga-104 portable transistor radio 120, *120*
Rigonda-Mono valve radiola 112, *112*
Rkacitelli wine labels 37, *37*
roly-poly dolls 82, *82*
Romantic portable transistor reel-to-reel tape recorder 116, *116*
Rozhki pasta packaging 29, *29*

S
Salhino Georgian wine label 34, *34*
Salut 21, *21*
Saperavi Georgian wine label 36, *36*
Sasha perfume packaging 52, *52*
Saturnas vacuum cleaner 193, *193*
scales 74, *74*
toy scales 85, *85*
scooter, Vyatka VP-150 230, *230*
Selga 405 transistor radio 115, *115*
sewing machines 68, *68*
toy sewing machine 85, *85*
sewing supplies box 61, *61*
Sfera 201 radio 124, *124*
Sgushchonka label *24*, 25
shaver packaging 55, *55*
Shilasis 405 D-1 portable television set 122, *122*
shoes 62–3, 175, *175*
Sirius 5 electric valve radiola 110, *111*
Skazka O Tsare Saltane: perfume

bottle 53, *53*
perfume packaging 54, *54*
Skazochnaya Azbuka fairy tale book 93, *93*
skis 97, *97*
Skorokhod shoes label 62, *62*
Slava table alarm clock 202, *202*
slide projector, Svet DM-3 212, *212*
Smena 8M scale focus camera 210, *210*
snowmobiles 153, *153*
soap packaging 176, *176*
social awareness posters 104–7, *146*, 147, 164–9, 194, *195*, 204, *205*
soda siphons 67, *67*
soda water vending machine 165, *165*
soft toys 83, *83*
souvenirs: Orbita souvenir box 197, *197*
souvenir paper bag 32, *32*
Sovetskoe Champanskoe Soviet 'Champagne' label 36, *36*
Soviet Life magazine *57*, 58
Sphinx super-functional integrated system 159, *159*
spice sets 76, *76*
Spidola transistor radio 117, *117*
Sport 2 movie camera 212, *212*
Sport 2 portable transistor radio 115, *115*
Sport Aeroflot Airlines sweet wrapper 13, *13*
Sport DIY knitted hat 96, *96*
Sport sweet wrappers 14, 21
Sputnik cigarette packaging 197, *197*
Sputnik wind-up shaver packaging 55, *55*
squirrel plastic toy 91, *91*
squirrel rubber toy 91, *91*
Start-3 television 122, *122*
Stolichnaya vodka labels 41, *41*
stove, toy electric 84, *84*
sugar bowls 64, *64*
Surpriz portable transistor radio 116, *118–19*, 120
Svema magnetic tape packaging 176, *177*
Svet DM-3 slide projector 212, *212*
sweet tins 196–7
sweet wrappers 12–21

T

table lamps 72, *72*
tape recorders 110–11, 116, 121
taxis, VNIITE-PT project *226–7*, 228, *228*
TDS-3 stereo headphones 124, *124*
tea tins 27, *27*
Technical Aesthetics magazine 216–19
Technika Molodezhi magazine 181, *181*
telephones 129, 160–1
televisions 122–4
Tetra Georgian wine label 35, *35*
tetrahedron-shaped milk carton 24, *24*
textile patterns 49, *49*
theatre construction kit 87, *87*
thermos flask 75, 176, *177*
ties 50, *50*
tins 27, 31, 33, 75, 196
tobacco packaging 44–5
Tonika electric guitar 201, *201*
tooth powder 27, *27*
toys 78–95, 141, *141*
Troika assorted confectionery box 33, *33*
trucks: three-wheel prototype 154, *154*
toy trucks 81, 90
Tula sewing machine 68, *68*
Turist 1 electric guitar 200, *200*
Tuzik chocolate wrappers 18, *18*
Tuzik sweet wrapper 12, *12*
Tvishi Georgian wine label 34, *34*
26 Bakinskikh Komissarov movie poster 134, *134*

U

UE4 portable iron 68, *68*
UP 1 vacuum cleaner 192, *192*
Ural 650 electric guitar 201, *201*
USSR athletic bag 99, *100–1*
USSR Metalloobrabotka logo and posters 185, *185*

V

vacuum cleaners 192–3
vases 64, *65*
Vecherinka movie poster 135, *135*
Vef-206 portable transistor radio 120, *120*
Veseli Zoosad chocolate wrapper 18, *18*
Vesennie Khlopoti movie poster 131, *131*
video tape recorder, Electronika 591 portable colour reel-to-reel 124, *125*
Vilia camera *210*, 211
Vkus Svezhego Vetra movie poster 166, *167*
VN10 UP4 desk fan 71, *71*
VNIITE-PT project *226–7*, 228, *228*
vodka labels 41–2
Volga GAZ-M21 *150*, 151, *151*
Vosmoe Marta sweet wrapper 12, *12*
Vostok 1 confectionery tin 197, *197*
Vostok 1 table clock 203, *203*
Vrema, Vpered! movie poster 134, *134*
Vremya Otdykha S Subboty Do Ponedelnika movie poster *136*, 138
Vyatka VP-150 scooter 230, *230*

W

Waiting for Instructions from the Centre (poster) *138*, 139
wall lights 73, *73*
washing machines 69, 192
toy washing machine 85, *85*
water heater 76, *76*
wine labels 34–7
wristwatch, Polot 204, *204*

Y

Ya, Babushka, Iliko I Illarion movie poster *137*, 138
Yava cigarette packaging 45, *45*
Yubileyny RG-3 portable valve electrophone 110, *111*

Z

Za Rulem driving toy 81, *81*
Zaichik mini-cart for children 85, *85*
Zenith Avtomat 208–9, *209*
Zenith camera mock-up 210, *210*
Zenith-E cameras 207, 208, *209*
Zhurnal Mod magazine *56*, 58, 60, *60*
ZIL KH 240 electric refrigerator manual 77, *77*
Zil-Sides VMA 30 fire truck 229, *229*
ZMM electric coffee grinder 75, *75*
Zolotoe Koltso beer labels 40, *40*
Zolotoy Yarlyk cocoa packaging 38, *38*
Zvezda 54 113, *113*

Numbers in *italics* refer to illustration

Picture Credits

Unless otherwise noted, all images are courtesy and copyright © Moscow Design Museum.

The objects, graphics and photographs used in the book are from the collection of the Moscow Design Museum and the following individuals and institutions: Valeri Akopov, Anton Artemenko, Ivan Borisov, Yelena Gerchuk and Igor Berezovsky, Thymen Kouwenaar, Krasnogorsk Mechanical Factory, Krasny Oktyabr Chocolate Factory and Museum, Alexander Lavrentiev, Daria Makarova, Vadim Markov, Svetlana Mirzoyan, Moscow Museum of History, Museum of Industrial Culture, Museum of Packaging and Advertising, Museum of Retro Automobiles, Khusnutdinov Nail, National Museum of Fashion, Petrodvorets Watch Factory, Polytechnic Museum, Azat Romanov, Russian State Archive of Literature and Art, Vladislav Selivanov, Vladimir Shapkin, Kirill Sukhanov, Tatyana Troitskaya, Vyatskiye Polyany Museum of Industrial Culture.

They also featured in the following exhibitions, curated by Alexandra Sankova and Alyona Sokolnikova: *Soviet Design, 1950–1980*, Moscow, 2012 (travelling) and *Red Wealth: Soviet Design, 1950–1980*, Rotterdam, the Netherlands, 2015 (travelling).

Quotations

The quotations in this book have been extracted from various Soviet posters of the period, with the exception of p. 184, which is credited to Yuri Gagarin in Simon S Utkin, *Essays on Marxist-Leninist Ethics* (1962), p. 180.

Acknowledgements

The authors would like to acknowledge the following people for their contributions to and support of the project:

Museum Team: Svetlana Chirkova, Olga Druzhinina, Natalia Goldchteine, Stepan Lukyanov, Ekaterina Shapkina and Yulia Voronkova.

Contributors: Valeri Akopov, Dmitry Azrikan, Aleksander Ermolaev, Mark Konik, Maria Maistrovskaya, Vladimir Runge, Yuri Soloviev, Alexandre Vassiliev and Igor Zaitsev.

For their assistance: Gleb Aleinikov, Nadezhda Bakuradze, Mikhail Gurevich, Natalia Khubieva, Dmitri Makonnen, Aleksandra Nikonovich, Valeriy Patkonen, Natalia Pozhidaeva, Andrey Silvestrov, Natalia Sokolnikova, Ekaterina Trubina, Nikolay Vassiliev and Danila Zinchenko.

Special thanks also to: Ksenia Akimova, Anna Amaspur, Peter Arseniev, Denis Babi, Anna Buali, Natalia Chakhmachan, Natalia Chechil, Tommaso Commonara, Ekaterina Danilchenko, Dennis van Diemen (Voerman), Anastasia Efanova, Emilia Faizulina, Lev Gelezniakov, Yelena Golysheva, Natalia Istomina, Sergey Kapkov, Dmitry Karpov, Olga Karpova, Olga Khaldeeva, Sergei Khelmianov, Anna Khitrova, Maria Kireeva, Igor Kochetkov, Alexey Konoplev, Irina Kostenko, Thymen Kouvenaar, Pavel Kuzmin, Olga Larina, Charlotte van Lingen, Marina Loshak, Daria Makarova, Ayuna Mitupova, Maria Naryshkina, Daria Obukhova, Dmitry Oktyabrsky, Elena Oranskaya, Tatiana Oskolkova, Elizaveta Ostrovskaya, Maksim Panfilov, Lyudmila Pavlova, Ella Pechechan, Jacques von Polier, Anna Prosvetova, Vincent van Rest, Diana Saimagambetova, Boris Saltykov, Elena Schneider, Natalia Sergievskaya, Pavel Shapkin, Tatiana Shovkun, Alexander Slesarev, Lyubov Sokolova, Tatiana Solovieva, Alexander Stakhanov, Evgeny Titov, Hans Wolbers (Lava Design), Igor Zabelin and Kira Zakharchenko.

Phaidon Press Limited
Regent's Wharf
All Saints Street
London N1 9PA

Phaidon Press Inc.
65 Bleecker Street
New York, NY 10012

phaidon.com

First Published in 2018

ISBN 978 0 7148 7557 6

A CIP catalogue record for this book is available from the British Library and the Library of Congress.

Commissioning Editor: Virginia McLeod
Project Editor: Robyn Taylor
Production Controller: Sarah Kramer
Interior Design: Villalba Lawson

Printed in China